OTHER BOOKS BY SUSAN FRIEDLAND

Marguerite, Misty and Me (Adapted for Young Readers)

Horses Adored and Men Endured: a Memoir of Falling and Getting Back Up

Strands of Hope: How to Grieve the Loss of a Horse

Unbridled Creativity: 101 Writing Exercises for Horse Lovers

Marguerite, Misty and Me

© 2023 Susan Friedland
Saddle Seeks Horse Press
All rights reserved.

Reproductions are with copyright permissions held by the University of Minnesota Libraries, Kerlan Collection of Children's Literature.

No part of this book may be reproduced in any form without written permission by the author, except in the case of brief quotations for articles, reviews or sharing on social media with attribution. The author encourages social media shares using the tag @saddleseekshorse.

Cover Design: Amy Summer Ellison
Photos of Susan and Knight: Carolyn Rikje
Illustrations: Bonnie Shields

Print Edition ISBN: 978-1-7327105-5-9
Ebook ISBN: 978-1-7327105-6-6

Susan Friedland
saddleseekshorse.com

Marguerite, Misty and Me

A Horse Lover's Hunt for the Hidden History of Marguerite Henry and her Chincoteague Pony

Susan Friedland

Saddle Seeks Horse Press

For Marlene, my sweet, horse-loving mother.

Today I make a jewel of a wish for each of you—
that someday you will write a book with living, breathing people in it.
You must make them so real
that forever afterward the mere mention of their names will bring them alive.

Marguerite Henry
Newsletter No. 6, 1968
Springtime at the Huntington Library

These are the events and conversations as best as I remember them.

Contents

Preface	IX
1. Writing Marguerite	1
2. Breithaupt Beginnings	13
3. Love in a Pine Forest	27
4. A Journalist's Journey	35
5. A Book, an Artist and a Pony	45
6. Mole Meadow and Mary Alice	59
7. File Folders, Paper Scraps and Author's Craft	69
8. Researching and Living the Story	79
9. Story Feedback from the Saddle	93
10. The Struggle of Bridling Pegasus	103
11. The Pinnacle of Success	111
12. Fan Mail and Friendship	123
13. Influence Before Influencers Were a Thing	133
14. Chincoteague Pony Superfans	145
15. Pony Penning Prelude	157
16. Swimming Ponies and Winning Ponies	171
17. The Misty Mystique	185

18. A Triumphant Life	197
19. Marguerite My Muse	213
Notes	231
Acknowledgements	247
Book Club Questions	253
A Note From Me to You	255
About the Author	256

Preface

In 2021, I discovered an autographed copy of the children's book Misty of Chincoteague for sale on Etsy. The inside page bore the title followed by Marguerite's cursive: "comes to Susan with happy wishes from Misty and Marguerite." On the opposite page was a hand drawn horse shoe and the words underneath read "Misty's autograph."

I already owned a copy of Misty of Chincoteague, and the price of this special edition was the equivalent of five riding lessons with my trainer! Was this a ridiculous splurge, or was this special edition meant for me?

When the treasured book arrived, I took a snapshot of the autograph and shared it in a Facebook group for equestrians. In ten minutes, it had two hundred likes and dozens of comments. In thirty-six hours, it had over two thousand likes. Apparently, I am not the only one who still loves Marguerite Henry, the author of Misty, of course, but also dozens of other children's books with horses at the center of their storylines.

As a writer, former history teacher, and a person with geographic ties to the area where Marguerite wrote Misty and several of her most beloved books, I immersed myself in research thanks to the Marguerite Henry Archives at the University of Minnesota and the fabulous opportunity to speak with people who knew and adored Marguerite. Here are a handful of highlights from my journey:

- Meeting the man who rode Misty three times a week with the author when he was a boy.

- Getting to know the illustrator who worked on Marguerite's last book.

- Speaking with Marguerite's next-door neighbor, a (then) little girl who let herself in Mrs. Henry's house through the open door and hung out with her.

- Locating her childhood home in what was then a German neighborhood in Milwaukee.

- Discovering her high school and college yearbooks.

- Reading the 1923 Sheboygan newspaper article detailing Marguerite's wedding to Sidney Henry.

- Reading hundreds of fan mail letters crisscrossing decades.

- Finding an unpublished manuscript on Miniature Horses.

Through it all I kept thinking, "Marguerite's life needs to be a story! It's just as exciting as the ones she wrote." And so here it comes to you with happy wishes from me and my horse Knight.

Tally ho!
Susan Friedland

1

WRITING MARGUERITE

I searched the built-in bookshelf by the fireplace in the room we never used, scanning a row of marriage and self-help books, then dog care books, finally landing on the horse section. The slate blue, hardcover spine and cheery yellow title font, were unmistakable. I slid the volume out from its position, and flipped to the title page, smiling at the illustration of a scampering pinto pony, mane and tail flying as a seagull soared above the marsh.

I missed you, Misty.

I plunged into reading *Misty of Chincoteague* for the first time as an adult. I had forgotten so much of the storyline. The adventure seemed both familiar and new. Reuniting with my storybook character friends Paul and Maureen and their Chincoteague Ponies was so heartwarming,

I had to share it on social media. Surely other horse lovers like me would also want to reconnect with this beloved horse story too.

A few days later—this would have been September 2018—I snapped a picture of page 82 and posted it on Instagram. The Wesley Dennis illustration at the end of Chapter 8 of Marguerite Henry's masterpiece shows a soaking wet stallion on the beach. The wild horse had just shoved a surprised Paul who is in motion, mid fall, arms up, about to land on his backside. At that moment I had no clue that the storyline of my life was about to set me back on my heels and I would be shoved out of the way, just like Paul Beebe.

***

As a horse crazy girl without a horse of my own, I found solace and inspiration in the stories of Marguerite Henry. Books like *King of the Wind, Brighty of the Grand Canyon* and especially *Misty of Chincoteague* somewhat satiated my desire to be close to my favorite animal. Through the wonderful words of Marguerite, I curried and cared for Sham in Morocco, and despite my fear of heights, navigated treacherous Grand Canyon pathways with Brighty. My favorite reading romp was galloping the Phantom, Misty's mother, along the Atlantic. From the comfort of my sunny yellow bedroom decorated with posters pulled out from horse magazines and shelves adorned with Breyer model horses, I adventured with my storybook horses: a resilient Arabian stallion, brave burro, and wild Chincoteague Pony.

When I was twelve years old, Cindy, a friend of my parents who lived five miles away and owned a few backyard horses, changed my life. Through her invitation, I graduated from loving horses in books to befriending them in person. Jim Dandy, the chestnut twenty-Quarter Horse I had the privilege of riding whenever I asked Cindy's permission, carried me through the open spaces and forests of Wayne, Illinois. Jim Dandy and I trotted through twisty trails of Pratt's Wayne Woods Forest Preserve and meandered through fields fringed by cattails and Queen Anne's lace. I've been smitten with horses ever since.

Somehow during those Wayne riding days, I learned my favorite author Marguerite had lived in this very town decades before I swung a leg over the saddle. Wayne was my happy place. Was it her happy place too?

***

The idea to hunt down the backstory of Marguerite flickered in my brain after a December 2018 book signing for my debut title *Horses Adored and Men Endured: a Memoir of Falling and Getting Back Up*. At the event hosted by Mary's Tack and Feed in California, where I lived at the time, I met Laura Murry, a criminologist. Laura shared with me how special book signings were to her, and it all started with meeting Marguerite Henry in Rancho Santa Fe when she was a girl. Laura unfurled a story that made my eyes widen and heart leap.

"It was such a special memory. My mom and I had been fighting. I was ten and petulant and pretty much an ungrateful child. I wanted to go home. My mom said, 'No! I think you're going to like this. You see that lady right there? That's the one who writes your favorite books.' I was waiting in a long line under the shade of a eucalyptus tree with a very well-dressed woman sitting at a table. To me an author was a mythical creature ... I asked my mom what I was supposed to do. She said purchase her book. It was *Black Gold*. I got the book. 'Now walk up to her and tell her thank you.'"

"I walked up, and I wasn't a shy kid, but I didn't understand the book signing thing. I introduced myself. She asked me what my favorite book was and did I have a horse. Her hair was perfectly coiffed—swept up on her head in a little bun. She had this grace and style about her, and I was just mesmerized.

"She was very soft-spoken and looked me right in the eyes. She was engaging to a child and so sweet. She wasn't bubbly, but demure. I felt like I was really special to be there with that lady at that time. To this day I love going to book signings. I just never forgot that experience—authors made these worlds for me. This probably happened in 1972, but I remember it like yesterday."

The details Laura shared transported me to the Marguerite Henry book signing. I felt Marguerite's warmth and respect by the way she asked Laura about her horse status and favorite book. As beautiful and special as Marguerite's stories were, it seemed she was a beautiful and special woman whose story had never been told. Perhaps I could dig in and discover the woman behind the books. It sounded like a fun endeavor and seemed like a way to make up for unfinished business subconsciously hanging over my head.

When I was a teenager in the 1980s, I found out one of my mom's friends, Mary Ellen Birchfield, had ridden the pony Misty when she was a little girl. I couldn't believe it. My mom told Mary Ellen how much I adored Marguerite and her book *Misty*. Later Mary Ellen gave my mom a black-and-white photograph of a little girl wearing a cowboy hat and a smug smile sitting aboard a palomino pinto. It was Mary Ellen when she was young, riding Misty! She also gave me Marguerite Henry's *Rancho*

Santa Fe, California address. My mom framed the snapshot of Misty and Mary Ellen, and I held on to Marguerite's address.

The cream page with blue cursive words bearing my favorite author's exact location overwhelmed me. I couldn't believe I possessed a link to someone so famous and revered! I had to reach out, but wasn't sure what to say. I longed to know and, probably without realizing it, be known by Mrs. Henry. However, as a shy girl with perfectionistic tendencies, I placed the treasure in my desk. I had strong intentions to one day pen a letter to my heroine. That day never came. Marguerite died at the age of ninety-five in 1997. The paper with the Rancho Santa Fe P.O. Box number remained hidden in my desk, my fan letter unwritten.

I thought more about Marguerite in 2019 as I replayed my conversation with Laura from the book signing. It seemed if Laura had such vivid memories of the author from a quick interaction, surely people who knew her from the neighborhood in Wayne when they were little kids might share their memories too. Maybe I would glean enough information to write a magazine article or two for the equestrian market. Although I was teaching middle school history in Los Angeles, I flew back frequently to visit my parents and sister in Illinois. With a little persistence, I thought I could connect with people in Illinois who knew Marguerite.

During that spring break trip to Chicagoland, my mom and I set out for the assisted living home where Mary Ellen now lived. My mom hadn't seen Mary Ellen in years. As my mom greeted Mary Ellen and introduced me, the pale woman sitting up in bed smiled and extended her arms for hugs. After our quick embrace, I held out the framed picture of her as a little girl aboard Misty of Chincoteague. Mary Ellen's face softened. I asked her about the pony, but she was unable to answer my questions.

She remembered her cowgirl outfit and how she met Marguerite through a friend of her grandmother's, a librarian named Mildred Lathrop. We stayed for a while and my mom and Mary Ellen chatted. I showed her pictures on my phone of my bay Thoroughbred gelding, Knight, and she said he was beautiful. I was disappointed to not walk away with fun facts about Misty, but I thought maybe it had brightened Mary Ellen's day to have visitors. Perhaps in that moment she needed a hug more than I needed pony trivia.

The next day, my mom and I stopped in at the police station in the Village of Wayne. The structure, about the size of a one-room schoolhouse, seemed a good option to begin my quest to track down people who knew people who knew Marguerite. I hoped since it was such a small town that officers would know which residents had been around for decades. Maybe they would help me? I introduced myself to the officers, mentioning I had learned to ride in nearby fields and across the street at the riding school. I added I was an equestrian writer and blogger seeking people who might remember Marguerite. As one officer made a couple of phone calls and grabbed a Post-It note to jot down some contact information, a man entered the station and started up a conversation with another officer. I recognized his voice.

It was Cindy's son—the woman who owned Jim Dandy, the woman who gave me an entry to the horse world in real life, just as Marguerite gave me entry through the pages of her stories. We laughed and tried to recount the last time we had seen each other, realizing it was in the late 1980s. He told me I hadn't changed a bit, which I knew wasn't true since I no longer wore purple eyeshadow or permed my hair.

I asked how his mom was doing, and he responded she had passed away several years earlier. I said I was sorry. I folded the Post-It with the contact's name, and shoved it into my pocket, as we reflected on what a spirited person his mother had been. I said I remembered how Cindy's preferred riding gait was the gallop.

Later I wrote a blog post tribute to Cindy—a delayed thank you for opening up the world of horses to me. As I reflected on her passing and about how I never wrote Marguerite my fan letter, a sense of urgency ignited in my heart. I had to find out what I could about Marguerite from the people who knew her, before they, too, like Cindy, no longer blazed about in the saddle.

***

Like Marguerite, I was a Midwesterner who moved to the promised land of sunny Southern California. She did so in her golden years, in the early 1970s, but I headed west while in my twenties in the late 1990s, for sunshine and a job transfer.

Unlike Marguerite, the Midwest beckoned me home twenty-five years later.

A few short weeks after my trip to see Mary Ellen and stop by the Wayne police station, my world turned upside down. My husband revealed he had been having an affair for two years. The man, now my ex-husband, had been keeping several secrets from me. His real life storyline dramatically opposed the "good guy" role he had played in *Horses Adored and Men Endured*, my debut book—my horse lover's dating memoir. The book had been just six months earlier. How embarrassing and crushing. Not just the infidelity. I had shared on social media and my blog snippets of our relationship and his comical status as a bumbling but affable horse husband.

I cringed, realizing our relationship history was irretrievable in my book, intended to be a fun and hopeful read. I could delete him from my blog and social media posts, but I couldn't delete him from the pages of print and ebooks. The book that I thought had been a work of nonfiction was now fiction—its happy ending had been overturned.

The first week living in the revelation's wake, I couldn't eat, barely slept, and the only moments of reprieve from the cruel truth were when I was with Knight, my retired racehorse-turned-riding horse. My saddle provided a temporary escape from sorrow. The tranquil scenes between Knight's perked brown ears—views of the tawny foothills of Temecula Valley, soaring eucalyptus trees and a leggy foal dashing around in his field as his dam grazed reminded me there was still beauty in the world.

Unfortunately, these moments were scarce due to urban sprawl and my conviction horses need daily pasture turn out. It was a seventy-five-mile commute one way through Los Angeles and Riverside County traffic to my haven, the farm where my Thoroughbred best friend lived. The total commute time was in the three-hour range.

While we worked with a mediation attorney, the man I had once loved brainstormed unorthodox ways to keep our Orange County home "for investment purposes" and stalled on completing the various legal documents that would officially sever our martial bond—a bond that had already been broken for years, apparently. Our house sold the week before the pandemic shut down. Six months after that, the day finally arrived when the dissolution paperwork was complete. I realized it was September 11, and thought it fitting.

I moved twice in less than a year. The first time to a tiny apartment to put geographical space between myself and my betrayer, and the second to gain a backyard so I could bring my dog home after living ten months with a dog-loving friend. It had been impossible to find a large-dog-breed friendly rental in the span of one week.

Neither of the rentals took me closer to my horse, and that was a problem. And after an almost complete school year of online teaching because of the pandemic, I knew one thing: I *had* to live closer to Knight and create a horse-centric lifestyle as a newly single woman. I had to make up for the previous decade in which my equestrian interests took a back seat in favor of family activities such as my step children's sporting events and afternoons at the beach (when I wanted to be at the barn).

After much prayer and discussion with family and close friends, I gave up the security of a job I had loved for twenty-two years and a work family I treasured. I headed back to a kinder, gentler, but as yet, unknown way of life in the Midwest. I needed a chance to regroup. My Florida-bred, California-raced gelding moved into a postcard perfect horse farm with green fields flanked by white wooden fences. It was less than a half hour drive from my folks' house where I had landed. I didn't really have a solid plan, but I figured I would make it up as I went along. All I knew was that Marguerite was part of my future.

During this transition time, an older gentleman happened upon my equestrian blog SaddleSeeksHorse.com. He found the picture of Mary Ellen atop Misty and read my blog post. He emailed thanking me for reminding him of happy childhood memories when he lived in Wayne. After an email exchange, we spoke on the phone. He said he wasn't at all horsey, but he remembered Marguerite and Misty living in his neighborhood. He gave me the name of a woman who would have known all the neighborhood kids when Marguerite and Misty had lived in Wayne, but he said he did not have her current contact information. At least I was one step closer to Marguerite.

As the new person at the horse farm where Knight became pasture pals with another bay gelding, I had many get-to-know-you conversations. After an August ride in 2021, I told a fellow boarder the condensed version of my story, complete with my desire to dive into Marguerite Henry's history. She knew of the woman with all the Wayne community ties and later sent me her email address. I dashed off an email explaining who I was and what I was doing to preserve the legacy of Marguerite. The woman responded quickly, kindly sending the email addresses of about a half dozen individuals who in the 1940s and 1950s played with the real life Misty and Brighty, frolicking in Marguerite Henry's pasture at Mole Meadow, her farm in Wayne.

Maybe I was home in Illinois again in order to preserve the memory of a woman I admired. An Internet search and Ancestry.com revealed Marguerite and her husband, Sidney Henry, had no children. However, I found a distant cousin of Sidney's in Sheboygan, Wisconsin, who was an amateur genealogist, and we became email pen pals.

As the weeks passed, I felt privileged to begin this deep dive into the life of Marguerite, but part of me wondered if this mid-life horse-related obsession could have been pacified with the purchase of a second steed, or maybe a truck and trailer. Had I attained a new level of horse girl weirdness? Was I eccentric or a historian?

I decided one of the best places to search for information on Marguerite would be at my local library, and set off to Gail Borden Library in Elgin, Illinois, which coincidentally was the same library where librarian Mildred Lathrop showed Marguerite a *Sunset* magazine article about the real-life burro she wrote about in *Brighty of the Grand Canyon*. This was the same Mildred who introduced Mary Ellen to the real pony Misty.

I approached a librarian to ask for help.

"I'm here to look up information in local newspapers on the children's author Marguerite Henry."

A wide smile spread across her face. "When I was in elementary school, I wrote Marguerite Henry a letter and she wrote me back. I still have it somewhere."

Surprise and hope swelled within me. Perhaps my exploration into the life of Marguerite would yield something positive, not just for me, and the community of like-minded blog readers I had gained over the years, but anyone and everyone who cared about books and children and animals.

As the months passed, with every thread to people who had a connection with her, every out-of-print book I scored from online booksellers, and every historical society and library I reached out to, I grew to know Marguerite Henry. With each informational tidbit gleaned about the people, places and practices that influenced Marguerite who influenced me, my thirst intensified to uncover more. My was to one day share her story with the world.

Much to my delight, I discovered Marguerite was a stellar human being, even better than I could have imagined. At just the right time, Marguerite Henry sauntered back into my life when I needed her most.

2

BREITHAUPT BEGINNINGS

Marguerite Henry was in a movie? How did I miss this when I was a kid devouring her famous horse books? There she was on my laptop screen, a slim senior with a tousled pixie hairdo retrieving a stack of fan letters from her mailbox. Marguerite narrated, "When I was a little girl, I wanted more than anything to have a horse of my very own. As I grew older, grownups said I'd get over my longing for a horse, but I never did."

I get you, Marguerite. I never grew out of that horse phase either.

It was 2021 when I viewed the surprisingly action-packed 1980 educational film about her writing process, *Story of a Book*. Marguerite researched in a library, jotted down notes, plinked keys on her typewriter, drove a Volkswagen van, admired a pinto in a pasture, then spied on her husband Sidney as he read a first draft of her manuscript on the patio.

If she noticed him looking confused or bored, she knew she had more work to do with her writing.

In the film, Marguerite had pep in her step, great posture and wore neck scarves in every scene. I sent a screenshot of my horse heroine driving her VW van to a friend, a graphic designer, who also grew up reading the Misty books. My friend texted back an altered version of the screenshot: Marguerite now drove the van wearing thug life sunglasses.

The film taught me that for every book, Marguerite worked through at least five different drafts and enjoyed, "revising and polishing a story. It's like grooming a horse to make it shine." After her manuscript had enough "grooming," she would send it off to her publisher. At that point, sadness would engulf her, until the manuscript was returned and she could dive into proofing and correcting typos.

A Google search revealed there was no shortage of sources to learn about the award-winning author Marguerite Henry, but I began wondering what her childhood was like. Could I find places and sources to help me create a sketch of a young Marguerite? What was she like as a little girl and teenager? What was her life like as a young woman and budding writer? Who was Marguerite Henry before she was famous?

For starters, I learned Marguerite was born in Milwaukee in 1902, to Louis and Anna Breithaupt. That was the same year my Grandpa Friedland was born. She was a Midwesterner, just like me. Cool.

A *Chicago Tribune* article revealed that when she was a girl, Marguerite's family owned a mare named Bonnie. However, things were complicated with the family steed. "I wasn't allowed anything to do with it. She was Bonnie by name and in appearance, but not in disposition. She had a habit of biting my brother in the breeches and leaving big teeth marks. Besides being a nipper, Bonnie was also a bucker and a bolter." I speculated whether or not Bonnie had equine gastric ulcers.

Fred, her protective older brother fifteen years her senior, never gave her a ride, nor did he even permit her to touch their horse. That seemed a bit extreme. But after his ride, he would "waft me into the air as if I weighed nothing at all." It's as though Fred understood his little sister's desire to ride, and he wanted to give her a way to soar. My guess is his toss was a safer alternative to riding.

Despite the fact the horse was a pill, the mare entranced Marguerite. As I found and read documents written by and about Marguerite, I discovered animals had mesmerized her since childhood. In a letter to a school district written when she was ninety-one, Marguerite described playing with her animals when she was a little girl, loving them so much she believed they would grow up and be able to talk. Placing them on her pillow, she would shut her bedroom door and go away for an hour, thinking upon her return, they would be able to speak "small words in a small voice." While Marguerite had a childhood pet guinea pig, unfortunately, she didn't specify if the animals she left on her pillow were real pets or stuffed animals.

Although her childhood animals never *really* spoke, the stories she wrote gave voice to horses, dogs, cats, foxes and a burro who speak to readers not in small words, in small voices, but in expressions and actions so memorable, the characters remain with us, twenty, thirty, forty, even fifty years after reading their tales.

I don't remember at what point I discovered the woman whose heart yearned for horses did not get her first one until she was in her forties, but I admired Marguerite for her tenacity in holding onto a dream and bringing books into the world that were so packed with joy. Both as a writer and a horsewoman, at fifty, I wanted to grow up to be just like her.

***

When I taught sixth grade history, we'd begin each new school year with a shoebox archeology project titled "Who Is This Person?" I would pass out one shoebox containing random items such as a Valentine from the 1990s, a brooch, an ashtray, an old newspaper clipping, a coaster and foreign coins to each table group. With great excitement, students would examine the box contents, list each item and its purpose (the ashtray always baffled them), then create a profile of the mystery person who owned the items.

My students loved this lesson, often creating sophisticated backstories on their mystery person including details such as age, ethnic background, gender, work, hobbies and even personality. At the end of the class period, they always begged me to tell them who their person was. It was a letdown when I revealed the truth: the artifacts in every box were all from the same person—a pack rat of a retired music teacher. I tried cheering them up by reminding them of the fun they had during the exploration and how they had sharpened their thinking skills during the lesson.

Eager to embark on my own, real-life version of "Who Is This Person?", I drove two hours northeast to the Milwaukee County Historical Society. I already knew Louis and Anna Breithaupt, forty at the time, welcomed Marguerite Anna, their seventh and final child, into the world April 13, 1902. Louis and Anna had two young sons who died, one before Marguerite's birth, one several weeks after her birth. In all her writings Marguerite describes herself as growing up in a family with five children. A few details of Marguerite's family life emerged as I scoured libraries and the Internet for her backstory, but I was hoping to find an old map or photographs or historical records that would shed more light on Marguerite.

Marguerite painted a merry little picture of her childhood in *Junior Book of Authors*. "We lived in a modest little home in Milwaukee and no youngster had a happier period of growing up. Marie, my oldest sister, made my dresses, embroidered and sashed in blue, and gave me music lessons. Elsie, a young nurse, taught me the doorknob method of pulling teeth and provided an allowance which was all the more exciting because of its irregularity. Fred, my big brother, used to take my hand and run with me, so that I flew through space in the most astounding manner, like a creature who could glide without wings."

Gertrude, five years older than Marguerite, was her personal dictionary. While reading Louisa May Alcott's classic *Little Women* as a young girl, Marguerite encountered the word "gingerly." She asked Gertrude what the word meant. Off the top of her head, Gertrude brought the word to life: "Papa has a drippy head cold, and this morning when he accidentally dropped his handkerchief, you picked it up very gingerly." As an adult Marguerite turned to Gertrude for input on her books, stating, "Editors could be wrong, but not Gertrude."

Marguerite inherited her love for words from her father, Louis Breithaupt, a man who recited poetry, Shakespeare and yodeled around the house. Louis was the president and owner of L. Breithaupt Printing Co. On rainy Saturdays, Marguerite joined her father at the print shop. The whirring presses and printed materials captivated her. She pretended to read proofs from her father's office, stating, "It was then, I think, the printer's ink got into my blood."

During the holidays, the Breithaupt family presented poems and staged original plays they had written for each other. One Christmas morning when she was seven, instead of a new doll, which would have been the common choice for a young girl's gift in the early 1900s, Marguerite received a writer's desk. It was a small red table outfitted with tools for an aspiring writer. Supplies included a cream pitcher containing sharpened pencils, scissors tethered with string to the table, paste, paper clips, a pencil sharpener and a mound of colorful paper from her father's office. Her father had written on the top sheet,

> *"Dear Last of the Mohicans,*
> *Not a penny for your thoughts, but a tablet.*
> *Merry Christmas!*
> *Papa Louie xoxo."*

The last o contained a doodled smiley face.

Young Marguerite reveled in words from her writer's station, tucked into a corner of the kitchen. While her mother and the Breithaupt's hired cook, a young German woman, meal prepped, Marguerite played with words. "While I scribbled and sketched at the little red table I was supremely happy. All about me were the most titillating smells and sounds—an egg whisk beating against its bowl, soups and sauces purring and boiling, the clink of clean knives and forks being dropped into their trays, and Mama and the hired girl chatting away about things that didn't matter to me. But what *did* matter to me was that they were there, and they were working too."

One such story written in the kitchen was a three-page drama about a pet frog. Marguerite caught the amphibian, gathered flies to feed him, built a frog-sized adobe house, and planned to find a frog wife for him. The ribbet-er jumped out of the house and escaped, but not without leaving a plotline for the young writer.

Marguerite's mother Anna, who wore "starched white shirtwaists and carried her head like a thoroughbred," read *The Delineator*, a journal of fashion, culture and fine arts published by the pattern design company Butterick. The magazine featured serial adventure stories and articles such as "Self-Confidence is Easy to Gain with this Home Furniture" and "Is Feminism Really so Dreadful?". There was even a column "Sewing School for Children." When *The Delineator* issued a call for children to submit stories based on one of the four seasons, Anna encouraged her youngest to participate.

Marguerite wrote "Hide and Seek in Autumn Leaves," based on a friend's birthday party recently held "in the country, in a wilderness of trees." When the children played hide and seek, Marguerite buried herself under a mound of crispy leaves, sure no one would find her. If it hadn't been for the birthday girl giving her dog one of Marguerite's gloves to sniff, Marguerite might have missed out on the party, her hiding spot was so stealthy. The hound sniffed her out just in time for cake and hot chocolate. Marguerite wrote the cake's frosting was so thick she wished she had the dog's long tongue to lap it up.

The Breithaupt family rejoiced with news that Marguerite's story was selected for publication. She received $12 for her work, valued around $350 today. In a congratulatory note, the editor suggested Marguerite should use the money to attend summer camp. The budding tween writer took her editor's suggestion to heart and registered for a church camp on Lake Pistakee in Northern Illinois. I tried valiantly to locate "Hide and Seek in Autumn Leaves," poring over issue after issue of *The*

Delineator online, pausing to read ads for corsets and Victrolas. I was more successful finding Lake Pistakee, about an hour from my home. I enjoyed lunch under an umbrella overlooking the water where over one hundred years ago, Marguerite splashed with her cabin mates.

Marguerite's Sunday school teacher, Laura Bertelson, doubled as camp counselor in charge of the gaggle of girls. One night around a campfire, she asked her charges their favorite hobbies. As Marguerite's fellow campers told tales of swimming, playing tennis and skiing, Marguerite felt sheepish, realizing all those hobbies were active pursuits.

With a dry throat she stuttered, "My hobby is words." Her shy proclamation was met with momentary silence. Then, as she was wishing to "'throw myself on the fire and turn to ash dust,' Miss Bertelson cried, 'What a coincidence! I like to play with words, too. What kind do you like, Marguerite?'"

Marguerite recalled, "It was too late now to become popular. I slid deeper into a quagmire of my misery as I confessed, 'tin-tin-nabulation.'" Laura acknowledged Marguerite's appreciation for *The Bells* by poet Edgar Allan Poe, smoothing out an awkward moment for the adolescent word lover.

It's possible Marguerite was not into tennis and skiing and outdoor sports due to recurring bouts of rheumatic fever from the ages ten through twelve. As a result, Marguerite stayed home from school for an extended period. During what could have been a lonely and boring chapter of life, she devoured books.

There was one at least one physical activity Marguerite was good at in her youth: roller skating. In fact, she made it a habit to roller skate every other day to Milwaukee's North Side Branch Library, a mile away from her home, to check out a new book and return the old one, "in whose spell I continued to live and breathe. Often as I flew pell mell to my destination I was still climbing mountains with Heidi, or wrassling wildcats with Dan'l Boone."

One day, as Marguerite roller skated to the library to return *Hans Brinker,* a Dutch tale about an aspiring speed skater, a motorcycle nearly ran her over. In order to avoid a collision, the driver thrust out an arm shoving Marguerite out of the way. She and the book landed askew. Her concern was not for her own scrapes and bruises, but for the precious book. She recalled seeing ominous warnings posted at the library about how defaced books would result in the patron losing library privileges. For a bibliophile, that was an unimaginable fate. She wrote, "What greater punishment could there be than to forgo a new book every other day? From the viewpoint of my scant years it would be far worse than a 'no vacancy' sign on the gates of heaven."

When Marguerite, sporting a head bandage, made it back to the library with the scraped up book, librarian Miss Delia G. Ovitz took her by the hand and led her to a glorious backroom—a book hospital. Miss Ovitz helped Marguerite repair *Hans Brinker.* "It was all like a doctor's office, but far more exciting. In this new and magical world I learned my first lesson in book-mending. Which I have not forgotten to this day. Every time I tape up a torn page I glow to my job as if I were Mother Teresa saving the human race."

Demonstrating an aptitude for book repair, Marguerite landed her first job thanks to Miss Ovitz. After school and on Saturdays, Marguerite mended library books. As a fan of Zane Grey Westerns *Riders of the Purple Sage* and *The Spirit of the Borders,* she began saving money from her job to buy her own ranch. Her dream ranch would have one stallion for each mare so the horses "would be as prolific as s so that fillies and colts would frisk about everywhere in wild abandon." That sounded like a worthy goal to me.

I wanted to retrace Marguerite's roller skating route and conferred with an archivist at the Milwaukee County Historical Society. First, he showed me the Polk City Directory, a thin-paged precursor to a telephone book. In the wide-spined, yet delicate century-old book I found Marguerite's childhood street address and an advertisement for L. Breithaupt Printing Co.: "Our printing is planned to attract and convince." I chuckled when the archivist approached my table, cradling the largest book I had ever seen, a Sanborn Fire Insurance Map. It looked like a movie prop.

He opened the massive book with a burgundy spine and gold embossed title—it spanned about four feet across the table—and flipped through pages. He eventually landed on the lot location of Marguerite's childhood home, and said that it was still a residential neighborhood, and chances were good the house was still there. Later that afternoon, I drove around the neighborhood. To my dismay, instead of Marguerite's house on that lot, I found a driveway next to a Victorian house with a mild Tower of Pisa lean.

Once the archivist and I found the location of the Breithaupt home on the map, we began searching for the geographic location of the North Side Branch Library Marguerite skated to and where she later worked. Although the building is long gone, we found a photograph which showed the library was in the same building as a natatorium—a public swimming pool. That cracked me up. Books and a dip, anyone?

With a flash of curiosity, I asked the curator if they had any old high school yearbooks from the early 1900s, and gave him a date rage. He disappeared for several minutes, returning with four Riverside University High School yearbooks from 1917 to 1920. Eager to see photos of Marguerite as a teenager, I began searching the Bs for Breithaupt.

I found the teenage Marguerite with wide eyes and dark wavy bobbed hair. I was overjoyed. Her name and photos were scattered throughout the yearbooks as she was active in several organizations. Her senior class picture lists her name and her nickname "Breity." Was this where she came up with the name for Brighty, the historical burro whose name in real life was Bright Angel in her book *Brighty of the Grand Canyon*?

During Marguerite's freshman year, she joined the Camaraderie Club, an all girls club with the stated goal of democracy, "the spirit which we are trying to inculcate into this large, friendly club … everyone is welcomed to the ever increasing band, from the tiny Freshman with golden curls to the dignified Senior in spectacles. At our meetings as at all other times, cliques are abolished, and all are on the same footing." The Camaraderie Club hosted parties once a month. Perhaps the open attitude and fun festivities planted the seeds for parties that would one day celebrate a pony's birthday. Besides her four years of involvement in the Camaraderie Club, Marguerite joined a Bible study club as a sophomore and served as president in her senior year, and during her junior and senior years she was in the drama club.

As a member of the yearbook staff, Marguerite wrote three pages of a fantastical class prophecy in *The Mercury*. One classmate became sultan of Hawaii, others made billions from finding a weeping willow. I didn't understand the inside jokes and references, yet I sensed Marguerite's confidence with words and exuberance in expression. She was in her zone. I read later that yearbook writing wasn't her only pursuit in high school. She tried selling grown up love stories to *The Atlantic* but they never got published. Even though she was active in school, and seemingly not shy, Marguerite once wrote she was very thin and wore multiple layers of socks to high school so no one would notice her skinny legs.

After admiring the Art Deco fonts and gilded designs of the yearbooks, I thought about the world events that happened during Marguerite's high school years: World War I raged and ended, the Spanish Flu swept through the country fomenting public debate on vaccines, and in 1920, the year she graduated, women got the right to vote with the ratification of the Nineteenth Amendment.

The archivist helped me track down Wisconsin State Normal School yearbooks—today it is the University of Wisconsin-Milwaukee. I found the collegiate version of Marguerite. She was a journalism student and member of multiple clubs. She served as vice president of the Dramatic Club and member of the English Club—a selective campus club only open to students with "special ability in literary appreciation and composition, as determined by the English faculty." She was also a member of the Pythia Literary Society and the French Club.

Again Marguerite wrote for the yearbook. An excerpt from her poem titled "Femininity" published in *The Echo* evokes images of a flapper, perhaps a woman she strived to emulate, and reveals her penchant for description.

> I mark the brilliant color of her cheek,
> The pretty, tilted snub of powdered nose,
> The childish treble voice, so soft and meek,
> The silken swish of super-stylish clothes.
> I note the bright cascade of bobbing locks,
> The charming smile of ultra-carmine lips ...

Wisconsin State Normal School's drama club staged *The World and His Wife* based on a 1920s silent film, heralded as "a Flaming Romance of Old Seville." Records don't show whether Marguerite had a lead role in the play, but she wrote she couldn't have her parents attend and see her smoking a fake cigarette.

Shortly after her time in college, at twenty, Marguerite got swept up in her own whirlwind romance, a romance that lasted a lifetime. I, on the other hand, was a late bloomer in the romance category and didn't find that one special person until I was thirty-eight.

3

LOVE IN A PINE FOREST

Pine trees standing sentinel stretched across the private ranch land as clusters of sage swayed. Within barbed-wire pastures, cattle chewed their cuds, unconcerned by the dozens of trucks and horse trailers parked along their fence line. *Not the Southern California most people envision*, I thought as I peered between two pricked chestnut ears during my inaugural ride as a member of the Santa Fe Hunt foxhunting club.

A few weeks earlier, a friend and I rode in a foxhunting clinic. Horses and riders of all ages and disciplines were invited to ride along to learn more about the sport. We learned the term foxhunting is a misnomer in California, and coyote chasing would be a more appropriate description. By riding at the ranch, the foxhunting crowd of horses and hounds serve as seasonal territory guardians, keeping coyotes at bay so cows can deliver their calves in peace.

I met Creole Rose, a pretty red Thoroughbred, sporting braids and wearing a halter over top of her snaffle bridle while tied to the side of the huntsman's trailer. I was trusting of this mare even though I didn't know her. The Master of Foxhounds who arranged this hireling told me Rose's owner was a woman in her seventies, and that both little kids and people who were out of shape had hunted the mare. He promised me that by the end of the day, I would not want to leave the saddle because she was the best.

I mounted and patted Rose's neck, trying both to form a bond and allay my nerves as we waited for the blessing of the hounds. A portly, white-robed Catholic priest read a prayer, and with a plastic water bottle containing what he assured us was holy water, sprinkled the hounds. When he stepped toward us, flicking the bottle, showering blessings on the horses, Rose took offense and shied away. I guessed the chestnut mare already felt blessed.

In a foxhunt, the riders are divided into three fields (groups). The first field rides fast to keep up with the hounds and jumps the pasture fencing. Panels strategically cover the barbed wire in the sections where jumping can occur. The second field rides fast but has the option to jump or enter the next field through the gates. The third field generally walks and trots, and doesn't jump. I joined the second field. The fieldmaster, our guide, led our group of about a dozen riders down a dusty lane at the walk as we watched the hunting staff in their scarlet coats, first field riders and the wagging tails of the pack eagerly sniffing and scampering.

Our group picked up the pace and trotted. Rose's forward stride caused me to post up and down at quick, comical intervals. A few of the horses began cantering along, so Rose opened up her trot to the point where I could no longer post, and I hovered in the saddle. Eventually

Rose decided cantering was easier, and I rode the waves of her gait as the open meadow narrowed into a shaded grove of pines. I was worried that she was too close to the horses in front of us. I wasn't sure how I could slow her down since we were moving at speed, and she kept ignoring my attempts to regulate her pace when I squeezed the reins, but Rose knew her job. When the horses ahead of us slowed, she automatically did too.

Under the canopy of trees, on a carpet of pine needles the color of the rust breeches of my youth, horses and riders paused to catch their breath. We took turns maneuvering our mounts in groups of twos and threes over to the water trough for refreshment. Two sandy colored hounds leaped into the trough for a quick cool off in between horses' slurping. The fieldmaster asked our group if we were doing okay. I was doing more than okay. I loved every minute of this riding adventure.

The footing changed from the wooded trail back to open pasture land. At the boarding stable where I kept my horse Knight, I was an arena rider who would grow concerned if I saw a spot at the edge where another horse rolled in turnout and made the footing uneven, or if after a rain, there was a slight puddle along the rail. On this wild ranch land, the ground was unmanicured, and the terrain varied. This was no challenge for the horses. They knew how to move.

Back in my rust riding breeches heyday, I had ridden Jim Dandy in a foxhunt once in Wayne, Illinois, as Cindy's guest. I was twelve. That hunt club was just down the road on the other side of the street from where Marguerite Henry lived. I wondered if Marguerite had ever foxhunted.

In the middle of our ride we were cantering along, and I realized a ditch sprawled on the path ahead of us. It wasn't a giant chasm, but a ditch, nonetheless. I had never jumped a ditch before, but we were moving so fast I didn't have time to over-analyze the ditch or get scared. Rose sprinted, and for a split second, soared. I giggled and declared, "I just jumped a ditch!" My eyes were wet, either from the wind in my face or the exhilaration, maybe both.

After the ditch, a short, steep hill, strewn with large rocks, lurked ahead of us. It looked impassable. Before I knew it, the whole group, including Rose and me, trotted and cantered up the hill. I would have *never* considered going up that hill if I were out on a trail ride with Knight. I didn't see a path; it looked impassable. These hunt horses navigated like mountain goats. "I can't believe we just went up that hill!" I'm sure some of the seasoned women I rode alongside were smiling at my newbie commentary.

Then we galloped. I couldn't remember the last time I had experienced the freedom of a gallop. It had been too long.

At the end of the ride when I reached the trailer and untacked the sweaty mare, I shared with the Master of Foxhounds how I laughed and cried and had a blast, thanking him for making it all possible. He replied, "This is the most fun a person will ever have on horseback."

As I reflected on the thrill of that ride during my long drive back to SoCal suburbia, I realized why that kind of riding made my heart sing: This is how I learned to ride! Before I took formal lessons with a trainer, my backyard riding lessons happened by riding Cindy's horses in Wayne. We walked, trotted, cantered and galloped and jumped when we wanted to, where we wanted to. And we didn't have a care in the world.

That day I fell in love with this friendship-forming, non-competitive, hours-in-nature way of riding, and I felt more like myself than I had in years. John Muir, the naturalist, once observed, "Between every two pines is a doorway to a new world." Astride a red mare, between rustling pines on a cattle ranch in the California mountains, I found a new world, and it was remarkably like that of my youth. Instead of feeling like a random horse-obsessed person in suburban Orange County, I felt like something bigger, part of a community of people whose hearts beat horse. Those galloping hoofbeats I first encountered on the pages of Misty thundered beneath me in real life, thirtysomething years later.

***

A male and female loon nuzzled each other's neck and chest as they rode the gentle surface of Lake Minocqua, Wisconsin. Their wavering tremolos, eerie avian laughs, broke the morning stillness as my companion and I arranged for our kayak rental. After back-and-forth phone calls to a local museum docent and emails with an attorney who wrote a Minocqua-area history book, I had enough clues to find the site where love sprouted exactly one hundred years ago between Sidney Henry and Marguerite Breithaupt.

On that overcast August day, we paddled past the private homes and docked boats that stood where Huber's resort, the Prohibition Era vacation destination had been. A lone bald eagle soared overhead.

In 1922, the summer after graduating from college, Marguerite joined her sister Gertrude and brother-in-law Russell on vacation at the recently opened Huber's Woodland Resort on Lake Minocqua in Wisconsin's Northwoods. Travel ads from the era billed Minocqua and its surroundings "The World's Most Concentrated Lakes Region," popular for golf courses, motor boating and, "natural bathing beaches with clean white sand." I've heard tales of fishermen in days of yore catching muskies over five feet long from the crystalline waters. The region continues to lure outdoor lovers to its pine forest paradise.

It's not clear how Sidney Henry, a hazel-eyed traveling salesman based in Chicago, crossed paths with the lanky word lover from Milwaukee, but the pair had an instant connection. The two fished together by day and danced to a pianist's plinking keys on a piano Marguerite described as in need of a good tuning. I envision them waltzing or dancing the polka, both popular with young people, a few short years before the Charleston craze.

David R. Collins, in his book *Write a Book for Me: The Story of Marguerite Henry*, described Sidney as a "tall and slender ... bespectacled young businessman [who] was clearly well read, with opinions based on fact gathering. He attracted Marguerite's attention upon their first meeting. They spent the afternoons fishing and sharing their thoughts and even their future dreams."

On their way home from the Northwoods, the Breithaupt party swung by Sidney's parents' home in Sheboygan, close to the shore of Lake Michigan, perhaps to keep the summer romance blooming. The Henrys' vegetable garden was at its peak, and the group had lunch incorporating home grown sweet corn and juicy tomatoes. As they said their goodbyes, Sidney and Marguerite vowed to reunite in Minocqua at the same time and place the next summer. A few weeks later, he showed up at the door of the Breithaupt home and met Marguerite's parents. The suitor's visit must have been positive, although her mother warned Marguerite that once a traveler, always a traveler. Undeterred, Marguerite dove headlong into a relationship with Sidney, eight years her senior.

The young lovers' engagement announcement appeared in *The Milwaukee Journal*, with a photograph of Marguerite, her wavy locks swept up revealing the nape of her neck, and a sparkling headband, perhaps of brilliant rhinestones, with a single feather plume adorned her head. She looked like a fashionable flapper.

Marguerite and Sidney married on Saturday May 5, 1923, and *The Sheboygan Press-Telegram*, Sidney's hometown newspaper, recorded the ceremony in vivid detail with emphasis on the clothing. I'm convinced the bride herself was the author.

"The bride's gown was of white georgette crepe with panels of beaded crystal and a girdle of braided silver. Her tulle veil fell from a coronet of pearls and crystals and she carried a shower bouquet of lilies of the valley, white sweetpeas and sweetheart roses."

Marguerite's bridesmaids wore a variety of colors and styles. Gertrude, her maid of honor, wore "pink and silver changeable taffeta, fashioned with a tight bodice and bouffant skirt caught up in front to show a flounce of silver lace." Both the mother of the bride and groom wore black.

On the day of the Henry-Breithaupt nuptials, the steepled and stained glassed First Baptist Church was "decorated with spring flowers. Two white arches wreathed in green mingled with spring blossoms spanned the space before the chancel, and from a large basket of spring flowers, streamers extended to the altar on which were decorations of spring flowers with large candles." Today a plaque on a children's playground commemorates the stone church that once stood, the site where Sidney Crocker Henry and Marguerite Anna Breithaupt committed their lives and love to each other.

A reception, with dinner and dancing, was held at the Hotel Astor in downtown Milwaukee; it oozed luxury. Guests might have glimpsed the vibrant stained glass dome, chandeliers, rooftop ballroom and retail spaces for both Rolls Royce and Lincoln automobiles. The Astor still stands, but has been converted to apartments.

According to the newspaper article, the newlyweds honeymooned somewhere in "the East" and then settled into a home on Sheridan Road in Chicago. Sheridan Road?! In the early 2000s I lived a few blocks from Sheridan Road when I taught middle school English at a charter school in Rogers Park. This north-south street paralleling Lake Michigan was a sought-after neighborhood in the 1920s and is to this day. The cool breezes of the lake, movie theaters, restaurants, department stores and public transportation on the elevated rail—the El—made the northern Chicago neighborhood a happening spot back then. Even Al Capone was on to it and purchased property in the area.

An undated Marguerite biography I found on Rand McNally letterhead stated Marguerite, "attended [college], intending to go into journalism, but romance altered her plans."

I later learned that statement wasn't entirely true, as Marguerite became a reporter and prolific writer for magazines. And the inciting event that set her career in motion resulted from trying to keep the peace at home. It reads like a romantic comedy storyline.

4

A Journalist's Journey

Before Marguerite became the queen of the horse book realm, she paid her dues ghost writing about famous business leaders for *Nation's Business* and *Reader's Digest*. In an odd twist, too many lamps received as wedding gifts helped launch Marguerite's professional writing career.

In a 1968 interview with the *Chicago Tribune,* Marguerite divulged she and Sidney, "received five lamps, so I bought five tables. I didn't want to hurt anyone's feelings by returning the gifts. Instead, it was my husband who was hurt and shocked by my extravagance. The only way I could make amends, I thought, was to pay for the tables myself. I had to have a job. Quickly. But all I could do was write."

The next day, the young newlywed walked into a magazine publishing office and asked for an assignment. She assured the editor if her writing was not acceptable, he could forgo paying her. The bold pitch worked, and soon Marguerite, twenty-two at the time, found herself on assignment packed into the middle of a crowd for the dedication of a new Chicago skyscraper. On July 7, 1924, former Kentucky Governor Edwin P. Morrow was dedicating the American Furniture Mart. At the time it was one of the world's tallest and largest buildings. The politician, clad in a three-piece suit, spoke from a bunting-festooned stage in front of the Lakeshore Drive building that cost $15,000,000 at the time of construction.

Perhaps because of the crowd, the impressive two million-square-foot building or maybe even the fact she was in the middle of her first paid writing gig since *The Delineator* published her story about playing hide and seek, Marguerite did not jot down enough content for an article. Determined her first assignment would not be her last, the aspiring reporter shoved through the throng to Morrow after the ceremony. She implored him, "Governor Morrow, this is my very first assignment and I can't remember half the things you said. If you'd only repeat the high spots so I could take notes!"

The Governor pulled out from his pocket a copy of the entire speech and handed it to her. Marguerite wrote the story, realizing, "All I had to do was boil it down. And that was fun. I've been boiling things down ever since."

Details are fuzzy on how long the young couple lived in Chicago, but from a career standpoint, the Windy City was a perfect location for a blossoming female writer in the 1920s. Their stay was long enough for Marguerite to launch a magazine writing career that laid the foundation for future fiction.

The next year Marguerite contributed a series of articles to *Photoplay* magazine's interior decorating column. Billed as "The World's Leading Motion Picture Magazine," the monthly periodical published stories of celebrities, movie synopses, fashion and home décor tips. My guess is Marguerite's article titled "Ornamental Lamps, Well Placed Add Beauty and Restfulness," was inspired by her honeymoon era lamp squabble with Sidney. In it she quoted silent film actress Phyllis Haver: "Lamps make rooms more livable and women more lovable." Marguerite wrote, "Just as the moon is more alluring when half veiled by a misty cloud; the sun's rays more wondrous seen through diaphanous raiment, so is a home made more beautiful by lamp light. The fascination of the camp fire isn't so much the leaping flames as it is the eerie shadows they create ... a room can scarcely have too many lamps and side lights, provided they are selected with careful taste." I would love to know if Sidney proofread this article and if so, what his reaction was.

Another *Photoplay* article Marguerite wrote praised the merits of wicker furniture and a third one "Use Picture Ideas to Beautify Your Home at Very Small Cost," was told through the storyline of a distraught friend named Betty Ann, a young bride, trying to settle into her new apartment with husband Bob and make it a home. Marguerite shares how she encouraged Betty Ann to amp up the style with her décor based on designs inspired by Hollywood sets. Were Bob and Betty Ann actually Sidney and Marguerite?

Learning that Marguerite's writing career was launched through magazines delighted me. My motivation to sell stories to publications wasn't to pay for tables on which to set lamps, but to develop a platform in the equestrian realm and to set the stage for writing books about horses.

My first assignment occurred not through a quest to keep the peace at home but through a Charleston dance contest in 2014 at an equine media conference—yes, such a thing exists—in Charleston, South Carolina. My sister Linda signed me up for the dance contest without my knowledge. I was not thrilled, but didn't want to disappoint the organizer of the event, and jetted to the ladies' room to practice the Charleston in front of the mirror. As I opened the door, I discovered a tall brunette, arms flailing, feet tapping, was already there practicing her dance moves. We giggled, and I showed her some new steps. I didn't win the contest, but the next morning during a speed networking event, I "won" the opportunity to write my first article for a horse magazine. The woman I danced with in the restroom was a magazine editor, and I had made an impression on her.

My debut article "Horses, Heights and Hollywood: a Sunday Ride Above Los Angeles" about a trail ride to the iconic Hollywood sign was published a few months later. That first story led to a follow up, and I have been writing horse-centric pieces for equestrian magazines ever since. One of my favorite "interviews" was with two-time Breeders' Cup Classic winner, Tiznow, the sire of my horse Knight. I met the legendary Tiznow at his Kentucky stud farm, but the interview was with his handler. I was enthralled by the dark bay stallion with a long, thick forelock, and elated to feed him a peppermint.

***

Eventually, Marguerite began ghostwriting for publications such as *System: The Magazine of Business*. She even contributed to *World Book Encyclopedia*. Marguerite did so much ghostwriting, she wrote an article in

1935 for *Writer's Digest* magazine titled "Adventures of a Ghost Writer." The essay shares Marguerite's methodologies for pitching stories, interviewing and writing articles. This seven-page personal narrative reads like a script from *I Love Lucy*.

In the beginning of the article Marguerite describes herself as a "a hard-working plodder about whom an analyst reported, 'no imagination;' one who knows deep down in her heart that no amount of mental shinnying will elevate her to the genus genius. But write she must!"

In order to get an interview, she would go in person to the potential interviewee's office and ask to see the man (because back then, it was always a man) by name. Actually, she didn't really ask. Marguerite would wear a fresh cut flower and tell the secretary she was Miss Henry there to see Mr. So-and-So. Nevermind that fact that she was married to Sidney Henry, and technically a "Mrs." not "Miss."

"The mystery of not knowing who the caller is or how she happened to select him to interview is much more provocative ... When a woman's name is presented, he likewise thinks of three things—a friend of my wife's; a school-day romance; or is that the one I met in the Bahamas! With two such delightful possibilities, he can do naught but see her!"

Wearing a flower and showing up at an office was just one technique. Dogged in her pursuit of an interview, she once waited on Milwaukee's Astor Hotel steps (the same hotel where her wedding reception was held) for an hour and a half to see incumbent Wisconsin Governor Walter J. Kohler on the campaign trail. He was scheduled to speak at a women's luncheon and was fashionably late. As a police escort accompanied him, "Mr. Kohler, like a ripe flower surrounded by sucking bees, tried to get out of his car and hurry into the hotel. I joined the swarm."

A campaign worker asked if Marguerite wanted to shake hands with the Governor. She meekly said yes. When introduced, she burst out with, "Don't you think that the industrial distributor is a very important factor in the economic scheme of things?" The Governor replied yes and then asked why. She explained she was writing an article for a publication and wanted to use his statement.

As he wove his way through the hotel to his spot of honor, Marguerite tagged along, peppering him with questions, thus gaining a complete interview. Later, the young reporter visited the Governor's grand private home in Kohler, Wisconsin, to get his statement okayed. During her visit she photographed the Governor, his wife and their gardens. She turned the trip to get her article signed off on into another story, submitting an article to a home and garden magazine.

In the article on ghostwriting, Marguerite asserts, "One thing that writing on assignment teaches you is that you can write any time, anywhere. And you don't have to be in a certain mood." Marguerite was on the fifteenth floor of a hotel in St. Louis during a 1927 tornado in which two hundred city blocks were destroyed. The lights and elevator went out and she had to walk down and up the stairs for a meal since room service wasn't functioning. Meanwhile, she was composing an article on grandfather clocks for an editor "seldom given to praise." The editor declared, "The grandfather clock piece was the most vivid thing you've ever done. Every one of your verbs conveyed action."

Another ghostwriting gig involved touring the Blatz Brewing Company in Milwaukee. As she learned the brewing process, proceeding from the bottle shed, stock house, carbonic gas rooms, keg-filling departments and more, each hospitable foreman from the varying stops on the tour would "proffer a cold, foaming stein of beer." Marguerite stated she was not aware the alcoholic content of draught beer was higher than bottled. Part of the job was to take photographs of the plant. She wrote, "In my 'mellow state' I saw picture possibilities in everything, so exactly twice as many pictures had been taken as the budget called for!" The editor only mildly rebuked her for the unnecessary photos. Estimates of the cost for photo processing in that era would be about $250 today. A mellow Marguerite snapped a small fortune in unusable photos.

Marguerite's calling was words, and Sidney's was sales. A World War I draft registration card for Mr. Henry reveals he worked in the Kansas Territory in "traveling sales" for Simmons Hardware. The Simmons company flourished in the 1920s, and Sidney worked for the company both in Chicago and later St. Louis. In fact, Census records show the couple living in a hotel in St. Louis in 1930, owning a radio and paying monthly rent of about $2,200 in today's dollars.

As a sales manager, Sidney's job required him to crisscross the country, frequently staying in one large city or another for a month at a time, and Marguerite ventured off with him. While away from home, Marguerite liked to try her at hand writing magazine articles in their new, temporary destination. During a stint in Philadelphia, Marguerite read a list of local publishers to Sidney. When she said the words "*Saturday Evening Post,*" Sid perked up, and encouraged Marguerite to call on them. At first Marguerite was shocked at such a suggestion, but then thought, "Why not?" The worst they could say was no, and she had heard those before.

"To Sid's lack of surprise and my disbelief, the *Post* bought a three-part series from me 'Turning Points in the Lives of Famous Men.'" Clarence Darrow was her most memorable subject, and the famed Chicago attorney grilled the young journalist during their meeting as though he were the one conducting the interview. Besides working on her own assignments, Marguerite frequently helped Sidney write sales bulletins. The couple used their individual strengths to bolster each other's careers.

Through writing, the future children's book author met and mingled with prominent individuals of her time. But the charm of children's stories soon eclipsed the allure of the famous.

***

Leaving urban life in 1933 for a small town in the middle of farmland set the scene for what would become Marguerite's long and prolific career as an author. Following the Henrys' time in Missouri, they rented a white cottage on a river in "Pretzel City"—Freeport, Illinois. Mr. Twist, the Freeport High School mascot, is a giant pretzel and a nod to the town's German roots. Corn wasn't the only seed planted in the fertile fields of Illinois; the storylines for children's book ideas germinated in Marguerite's mind. She also met the first individuals whose stories would be literary gold for boys and girls, as well as befriended an acclaimed illustrator who lived nearby.

Gladys Rourke Blackwood, a Freeport neighbor, graduated with honors from the Art Institute of Chicago, and during the 1930s, had a gallery on Chicago's fashionable Michigan Avenue. Gladys was an early pioneer of the art of the paper doll, with her paper dolls from the 1930s and 1940s selling today as collector's items. The illustrator, who had a disability that only allowed her the use of one hand from the time of her birth, also created art for greeting cards and wrapping paper. The iconic (but now extinct) Chicago department store Marshall Fields purchased one of Gladys' exclusive designs.

While living in the cottage, the Henrys hired Effendi and Beda Walkeala as their handyman and cook. As Beda baked bread and Effendi whittled small flowers out of blocks of wood, the Finnish husband and wife duo shared adventures of life growing up in the old country. Marguerite listened intently. One tale dazzled her so completely, she wrote a short story based on the events.

In *Auno and Tauno: a Story of Finland,* her debut book, Marguerite merged the Walkealas' story with Blackwood's illustrations. Children's publisher Albert Whitman published the 1940 picture book with a selling price of $1. Twins Auno and Tauno are a sister and brother who ski to school, gliding past reindeer while carrying herring in their lunch bags. The family's gray horse, named Tapio, pulls a sleigh, transporting them through the snow with the Northern Lights dazzling in the winter sky.

According to her older sister Gertrude, "American children at once responded to the story of the two little Finns, and suddenly Marguerite knew that writing for children was the kind of writing she had always wanted to do. She has a oneness of feeling with young things, human or other-wise."

In 1940, Saalfield Publishing released *Dilly Dally Sally,* a story based on Marguerite's own childhood as a girl who was easily distracted, which was also illustrated by Blackwood. In 1942, the team of Blackwood and Henry followed up with *Geraldine Belinda*, the short tale of a stuck-up girl and the consequences she faces from her character flaw. In 1943 they released *Their First Igloo,* co-authored by Barbara True.

At thirty-eight, Marguerite Henry had found her niche, embarking on a six-decade career in children's literature.

5

A BOOK, AN ARTIST AND A PONY

All her life, Marguerite Henry longed for a horse, but she did not fulfill the horse ownership dream until she was forty-four. Marguerite's long-awaited first horse, a pony really, became my dream horse and the dream horse of countless readers of *Misty of Chincoteague*. Published in 1947 by Rand McNally, *Misty of Chincoteague,* Marguerite's Newbery Honor-winning story about a brother and sister and a mare and her foal has sold over a million copies. It continues to enchant readers today.

I didn't realize that *Misty* was a work of fiction until I re-read it in 2018 and did some online research as I wrote my blog post "Misty of Chincoteague: Rereading a Classic Horse Book as an Adult." The story of the golden pony is based on real people (the Beebe family) and actual events, but some ideas and plot points were derived from Marguerite's imagination. In case it's been awhile since you've perused *Misty of Chincoteague* and its related books *Sea Star* and *Stormy, Misty's Foal*—or perhaps you've not yet read the three titles—here's a quick overview.

Misty of Chincoteague is set in the 1940s on Chincoteague Island, Virginia. Paul and Maureen Beebe live with their grandparents at Pony Ranch. Although they have dozens of ponies right outside their door, and they help their grandpa gentle and train foals to be sold, the children want a pony of their very own. They desire one to love and keep forever.

On nearby Assateague Island, which acts as a protective barrier to Chincoteague, a lighthouse rises like an obelisk above the pine trees, and wild ponies roam. The ponies exult in their freedom all year except during Pony Penning Week every July. That's when the horsemen of the Chincoteague Volunteer Fire Company round up the rainbow of pintos, chestnuts, palominos, buckskins and bays. The Saltwater Cowboys usher the herd across the channel separating inhabited Chincoteague from its wildlife refuge neighbor. Maureen and Paul hear stories of the Phantom, a mare described as "a piece of wind and sky." The Phantom somehow always avoids the pony roundup. The elusive mare steals their hearts, and they decide they must purchase her. Paul and Maureen keep this plan a secret from their grandparents and start earning money by gathering oysters and treading for clams.

Paul rides with the roundup men on Assateague on Pony Penning Day and happens upon the Phantom, glimpsing a silver flash of mist trailing behind her. He realizes it's a newborn foal. When the dam and filly are driven into the channel with the scores of other swimming ponies, the foal Paul had by then named Misty struggles to keep her head above the churning water. The boy heroically leaps off the boat ferrying him and his mount Watch Eyes across the channel. Paul swims alongside the vulnerable filly, ensuring her safe passage.

The next day, the fire company holds their auction at the carnival grounds, where the foals are purchased and taken to new homes. There's a dramatic moment in *Misty of Chincoteague* when it appears the mare and foal of the Beebe children's dreams will go home with a father and son from Norfolk. But alas, the folks from Norfolk win a different foal through a raffle. Thus the Phantom and Misty join the Beebe family.

Maureen and Paul train the Phantom using a bedsheet as a surcingle and a bag of rice on her back to mimic the weight of a rider. The mare goes along with her domestication, becomes a riding horse and even wins a race. However, Maureen notices she often leans out over the fence looking away toward the sea—toward Assateague. In contrast to her mother, the foal Misty is curious and friendly, readily accepting the world of humans. In the end, an empathetic Paul releases the Phantom back into the wild where she reunites with Pied Piper, her stallion love. The children's sadness of setting the Phantom free eases with the antics of their adorable weanling friend Misty. Her personality is so big that she is like a funny little sister.

This story enchanted its readers, and fans begged Marguerite to write a *Misty of Chincoteague* sequel. Since the book closes with Misty still a foal, it provided the perfect setup for new pony adventures. But Marguerite had no intention of writing such a book. Instead, she believed children could dream up their own wonderful sequels. Her resolve to never write a sequel was overturned, however, when she learned a lone foal was found nuzzling its dead mother on Assateague. Marguerite sprang into action and composed the story *Sea Star: Orphan of Chincoteague*, a book she later referred to as a PostScript to *Misty*.

The plot of *Sea Star*, published in 1949, centers on movie makers offering to buy Misty so she can star in a film and tour around the country to connect with children, many of whom had never met or petted a pony in real life. Maureen and Paul are torn between dutifully accepting the offer, as it will help finance their uncle's college education, or keeping Misty for themselves. The children consider the difficult decision as they gather oysters on Assateague for Grandma Beebe. Mid oyster gathering, the siblings stumble upon a bay orphan colt standing near his lifeless mother. The children cleverly catch the foal by shooing him into the water. Once the pony was deep enough in the water where he couldn't get away, Paul lifted him into their boat and the children brought him home to Pony Ranch.

The third book starring Misty was *Stormy, Misty's Foal*, with a storyline based on the deadly 1962 Nor'easter known as the Ash Wednesday Storm. By then, Marguerite had returned Misty to the Beebe family in real life so she could be bred and have foals. Also in real life, the now-celebrity pony was pregnant and due to foal any day while the storm pounded the Mid-Atlantic coast. Helicopters evacuated Chincoteague residents to the mainland. Prior to their airlift to safety, the Beebes led Misty out of her stall which was three feet deep in water, up the steps into their home, and into their kitchen. They filled the sink with water to serve as a trough. A mound of hay and a barn cat were Misty's companions as she safely rode out the storm in the kitchen. The family's quick thinking and resourceful plan saved the celebrity pony. When the family returned a few days later, Misty seemed none the worse for wear. She had opened the refrigerator and helped herself to the molasses jar and had chewed the edge of the Beebe's new wooden table that had served as a stall door to keep her out of the rest of the house. Misty was then trailered to a veterinarian's farm on the mainland of Virginia, where she delivered a chestnut and white filly aptly named Stormy.

Marguerite was with Sidney in Vienna, Austria, researching the Spanish Riding School for her forthcoming *White Stallion of Lipizza* as the Ash Wednesday storm raged. While reading a New York newspaper over breakfast, one sentence leaped out at her: "Misty, the pony of storybook and motion-picture fame, has been brought into the kitchen of the Beebe family to have her foal." The Henrys changed their travel plans immediately, and booked a flight back to the U.S.

Marguerite had to check in on the people and ponies she loved in person and had formed a special relationship over the years during her many trips to the island. Within twenty-four hours, the author was in Virginia at Misty and her new filly's side.

The Ash Wednesday Storm left death and devastation in its wake. Over three hundred fifty thousand birds, over one hundred ponies and forty people died. The Beebe family alone lost dozens of their personal herd.

Marguerite cleared her schedule to focus on assisting the islanders. In a cancellation letter written a month after the storm, Marguerite explained, "Chincoteaguers really are dependent on the ponies to bring tourists to the island so a Misty Disaster Fund has been started by people who love Chincoteague and want to make it possible for the oldest round up in American to continue. 20th Century Fox has very generously offered their motion picture of *Misty* to theaters all over the country who want to give a benefit performance. It is hoped that enough money can be raised to buy back the ponies that have been sold the past few years on Pony Penning Day and, in this way, reestablish the herds over on Assateague Island." The movie benefit plan worked, and the one hundred fifty wild ponies on the Virginia side of Assateague Island are thriving today.

Billy Beebe, grandson of Grandma and Grandpa Beebe, first cousin of Paul and Maureen, who owns the Beebe Ranch at the time of this writing, once said the book *Misty* was seventy-five percent fiction and the book *Stormy, Misty's Foal* was twenty-five percent fiction. Regardless of the percentages, the beloved stories from my childhood resonated as true in my heart.

***

The Misty I fell in love with when I was in elementary school would not exist were it not for a polo player from the East Coast. In the early 1940s, Marguerite was on a quest to find the world's finest horse artist for her first horse book about the founding sire of the Morgan breed. She searched library shelves for illustrator options and narrowed it down to her two top picks: Will James, the Canadian author and illustrator of the 1927 Newbery Medal-winning *Smoky the Cowhorse*, and Wesley Dennis, who had written and illustrated a 1941 picture book titled *Flip*. Set on a Kentucky horse farm, *Flip* is the story of a persevering foal who tried and tried to leap a stream in his pasture. Marguerite learned James was deceased and that Wesley lived over seven hundred miles away.

Sidney suggested Marguerite reach out to Wesley regardless of the distance, and she sent the manuscript of *Justin Morgan Had a Horse* to him. The author and artist arranged to meet in the reading-writing room of a hotel near Central Park in New York. As Wesley entered the room asking if Marguerite was Marguerite Henry, he blurted, "I'm dying to do the book, and I don't care whether I get paid for it or not."

Marguerite once wrote that besides their mutual love for animals, the two were "as different as two people could be"; however, the author and artist hit it off from the start. Their debut book, *Justin Morgan Had a Horse*, was published by Wilcox and Follet in 1945. Over the course of twenty years and fifteen titles, the duo became a children's book publishing dream team. Marguerite shared book royalties with Wesley and the two would go to schools and book fairs to deliver "chalk talks." As Marguerite spoke about their stories, Wesley would simultaneously draw the characters on a chalkboard or large pieces of paper. Some of those drawings on paper that entertained young audiences over fifty years ago are owned by collectors today.

Originally from Cape Cod, Wesley, a year younger than Marguerite, loved playing polo, point-to-point racing, and foxhunting. Wesley's study of horse anatomy occurred when he groomed horses for the National Guard and later as he scrutinized the equine form in Parisian butcher shops (since horse was not uncommon in French cuisine), during the year he studied under a French animal artist. Wesley's knowledge as a horseman and dedication to learning enabled him to dash out drawings with realistic movement and accurate mood. His charcoal and brush strokes on paper breathed life into Misty, Sea Star, Stormy and dozens of other equine friends and human characters, making them unforgettable.

***

Marguerite entered the world of horse ownership in order to write what would become her first horse story for Chicago publishing house Rand McNally. I like to picture her telling Sidney she needed a horse "for research purposes." The following is the history of the real-life Misty who became world famous and lives on today as an icon. Contrary to what the story of *Misty of Chincoteague* tells of the origin of its title character, Misty was born in 1946, not as a wild pony on Assateague, but on the ranch of Grandpa Beebe, the horseman and patriarch in the Misty book.

A palomino pinto foal Marguerite encountered during her first research trip to Chincoteague captured her heart and imagination. "The first time I saw Misty, the tiny filly ... was new as the morning and silky as milkweed floss."

Marguerite's travel companion, Wayne horsewoman Blondie Coffin, was tasked with the role of helping Marguerite select a suitable pony to bring home. There is no indication from archival documents or personal accounts that Blondie had any say in Marguerite selecting Misty. The writer laid eyes on a silver and gold foal lying beneath her mother and she instantly fell in love.

The deal struck between Marguerite and Clarence Beebe, the man simply known as Grandpa Beebe in the storybook, was that once weaned, the filly would be shipped to Illinois to live with Marguerite and serve as her writing inspiration. They agreed Misty would eventually return to the Beebe Ranch to be bred and have foals. Marguerite and Grandpa shook hands and with $150 paid by Rand McNally, the pony became Marguerite's.

The Henrys did not yet have a barn on their two-acre property in the Village of Wayne, but that didn't stop Marguerite from getting the pony.

Her neighbors, the Quayle family, agreed to let Misty stay in their barn. Misty arrived in St. Charles, Illinois via train car on a cold November day in 1946, the year before the book *Misty* debuted.

A Pictorial Life Story of Misty, published in 1976, retraces the earliest moments of Marguerite and Misty as a pair, showing a photograph of a bundled-up Marguerite sitting in deep straw, cradling the just-weaned filly's head as she slept.

Upon the foal's arrival, Marguerite and her neighborhood friends were concerned the shaggy creature wasn't the same filly selected just a few months earlier. In fact, Sidney teased Marguerite about Misty's appearance, stating she looked like a Siberian goat. Marguerite turned her head to hide her tears, wondering if Grandpa Beebe had sent her the wrong pony. Her thick winter fuzz lacked the golden vibrance of her newborn coat. Nevertheless, the weary filly who had spent four days on a train in a standing stall of a crate needed TLC. Despite what Marguerite considered a mix up, she was determined to care for the filly with a runny nose who barely ate a few bites of hay.

Marguerite spent the night in the Quayles' barn in the stall with the fuzzy newcomer. "She needed a live, breathing presence in the dark and I'd be there for her." With a blanket wrapped around her, as raindrops tapped on the roof and an owl trilled *whoo, whoo*, Marguerite tried humming to elicit a response from her. The pony ignored her all night. However, as the inky blackness gave way to gray morning, Marguerite heard the rustle of straw. Misty approached her! She lay down next to Marguerite. "Her whiskers brushed my palm, then her muzzle was cradled in my hand ... Her animal warmth felt good as she squirmed closer. I was no longer cold. The rain stopped, and we slept."

When spring arrived and Misty's winter coat shed out, the unmistakable white marking on her withers resembling a map of the United States appeared, as did the patch on her right side "in the shape of a plow, strangely like the state of Virginia." Grandpa Beebe had indeed shipped the right foal. A local horse trainer, Eddie Pacuinas, started Misty to be a riding pony. Besides being trained to ground drive and later accept a rider, Misty learned tricks. The Henrys taught her to extend a hoof in a horsey handshake and to step her two hooves on a stool and pose.

As *Misty of Chincoteague* book royalties rolled in, a three-stall barn was constructed in 1948. In the wake of *Misty*'s success, the real Misty blossomed into a media celebrity appearing at schools, libraries, book signings and parties. Marguerite planned elaborate birthday celebrations for Misty, documenting one in a six-page birthday party scrapbook from July 20, 1948. I paged through the scrapbook bound with a ribbon featuring a headshot on the cover of Misty as a foal while researching the Kerlan Collection Archives at the University of Minnesota. The first page begins, "Whee! I am 2 years old today. My birthday began with a hearty handshake." Marguerite wrote all the captions from the filly's point of view.

A photo of Marguerite and the hooved birthday honoree facing each other, just inches apart, shows Marguerite gripping Misty's pastern in a handshake. Its caption reads, "Notice the map on my withers. Shows up quite plain here, doesn't it?" The next page says, "I had a party. You should have seen the presents! There were carrots scrubbed clean (even the greens were washed), and a box of sugar lumps, and a bundle of hay and a sheaf of green oats tied with a gold ribbon." The thin blade topped with oats sporting a small ribbon near its base, is still taped to the page.

After opening presents wrapped in paper covered with galloping horses, several of the children rode Misty. Three pictures show little riders aboard the pony bareback, accompanied by captions stating, "Everybody was so darn nice about my day that the least I could do was to offer a few free rides. I did a little bucking and kicking so they'd know there was wildness in me. The grownups who watched thought it was maybe a gnat in my ear or horsefly. But it wasn't at all. I'm wild I am! I wanted the children to get a kick out of it."

The last page of the scrapbook is a signed guest list with the names of eleven neighborhood children, some penned in cursive, some in giant scrawling letters of those learning to write. The average age of attendees was six and a half years old.

Mary Jon "Jonnie" Quayle was one of the party attendees. When we first spoke on the phone Jonnie said, "I loved Marguerite Henry!" She said that when she was around five, she would go to Marguerite's house all the time. She wouldn't knock, she would just walk right in.

She also informed me she was the first person who ever "rode" Misty. You can see the 1946 photograph of the future equestrian in *A Pictorial Life Story of Misty*. The image shows Sidney Henry holding up a little girl bundled in winter layers over top of the filly who would one day become a celebrity. Even though Jonnie was the first person atop Misty, she said she didn't ride Misty at the birthday party commemorated by the scrapbook, as the pony was too green.

Jonnie painted a picture of her hometown and her author friend. "Wayne was just heaven to grow up in. Everyone in Wayne had a horse, that's the way it was. Misty stayed in our pasture. My sister Nancy and I would hop on and ride her bareback without permission. She wasn't famous then ... she was just a little horse growing up in our pasture with our other horses."

"Mrs. Henry ate at the country club for breakfast, lunch, and dinner, and I once asked my mother, 'How come we don't get to do that?' My mom said, 'She's famous. Mrs. Henry doesn't have children, so she doesn't need to make the meals.'"

When I asked Jonnie if she knew Mrs. Henry was famous, she replied, "No, I just knew she was this wonderful, nice lady who lived next door and that they always got to eat at the club. And she used to pay me a quarter to make her bed!" Jonnie laughed and wondered aloud if Marguerite unmade the bed in order to give her something to do.

Jonnie recalled Wesley Dennis at Marguerite's, sketching Jiggs the burro for *Brighty of the Grand Canyon*. Jonnie took home the drafts of Wesley's art that were deemed unusable, intended for Marguerite's trash bin. She still has them to this day.

Early in my research, I found a 1951 Rand McNally and Company ad promoting the book *Album of Horses* in the *Chicago Daily Tribune*. It posed the question: "What makes Marguerite Henry's books about horses so popular with children?" Beneath the question is a photograph of a smiling Marguerite, with her right hand waving hello from atop Misty whose front hooves are planted on a small wooden stool.

The ad continues, "Marguerite Henry has what her sister calls her 'feeling of oneness with young things.' She never writes or talks down to children. Whether she is currying a colt or chatting with a ten-year-old, she treats each with affection and respect. You can get some idea of her popularity with children from the fact that the neighborhood boys bicycle eight miles for the 'privilege' of cleaning her stable. One suspects that the secret of her success in writing about horses comes of having been born an unusually nice human being."

I felt the warmth Marguerite exuded, and I wondered about the identity of the neighborhood boys who clamored to clean stalls. Would our paths ever cross? I wish I had met this unusually nice human being. I had so many questions to ask her about horses and herself. I know we could have been friends.

6

MOLE MEADOW AND MARY ALICE

When I learned of Marguerite's heavy heartedness of living a horseless childhood, it totally resonated with me. In elementary school, when I wasn't reading one of her books, writing horse stories or playing with Breyer model horses, I galloped around my backyard pretending to ride a horse. I jumped over an upside-down picnic table bench with a broom placed in the X of the legs. Changing leads, I cantered from tulip tree to burning bush, then to the far corner of the yard to circle the aspen tree and dash back to my starting point. I also started saving all my paltry allowance money, combined with more lucrative birthday and Christmas cash gifts, so that one day I could buy a horse of my own.

One summer in the early 1980s, our family friend Cindy invited me to help exercise her mounts. Her herd included Odessa, a sporty bay mare; Peanut, a lanky, Roman-nosed chestnut; and of course, Jim Dandy, the senior bald-faced Quarter Horse who wore a Kimberwick bit. He had the hardest mouth of any horse I've ridden in my life.

Thanks to Cindy sharing her horses, I befriended several other horse-crazy teens who boarded their horses in her pastures. Our days were filled with riding adventures. There were trails to be explored, jumps to be sailed over, and wild black raspberries ready for tasting. With a few dollars in our pockets, we would ride to a small general store, take turns holding each other's horses and go inside to order deli sandwiches and pick up a bottle of pop. We had informal pony picnics just outside the small business that would have been walking distance from Marguerite's home at Mole Meadow, had she not already moved away to California.

Depending on the season, the purrs of the red-winged blackbird or raucous trumpets of Canada geese followed us as our troupe rode for hours through the glory of the Pratt's Wayne Woods. One summer we rode bareback, swimsuit-clad, to a swimming hole. We trekked along the Prairie Path, a trail converted from a third rail line, paralleling Dunham Road for a couple of miles. Then we crossed the road, and turned down a narrower, private road, that was flanked by trees and continued on the bridle path.

The homes we trotted by en route to the swimming hole were the stuff of horse girl fairytales, and a far cry from my family's small ranch house. Two-story colonial residences rose from vast, verdant lawns. Several of them had small barns with exterior design style mimicking the grand houses to which they belonged. Riding arenas with colorful jumps dotted several of the properties. I knew this was what heaven must be like (except for the horse flies).

We crossed the edge of someone's property line to another path leading to a grove of maples and oaks, which led us to a small pond. The secluded swimming hole shone like a mirror, but not for long. My riding companions sloshed into the water. Their horses willingly plunged in and my friends erupted into giggles and shrieks as they became swimming centaurs. I followed suit, nudging my steed's copper sides with my bare feet.

Jim Dandy good-naturedly joined in the frolicking. When he was in deep enough, the water covered his back. My legs slid out behind me, and I grabbed his chestnut neck in a bear hug to stay aboard. Just as I was getting the hang of this new way of swim-riding, he submerged his head. By the time my brain processed what I was sure was ensuing danger, his head and neck shot up. This companion I had known and loved as a horse transformed into something almost otherworldly, a creature part whale, part marine dinosaur.

I couldn't imagine Jim Dandy had been in a swimming hole before. How did he instinctively paddle his legs once the water was deep enough, and have no fear? I remember being terrified when I took swimming lessons at the YWCA when I was four. From whence did his seahorse skills derive?

***

If the story of wild ponies who swim in the sea had not attracted the attention of Dr. Mary Alice Jones, *Misty of Chincoteague* would likely not exist. Mary Alice had written ten religious books for children published by Rand McNally when Bennet Harvey, vice president of Trade Publishing, offered her the job of children's book editor in 1944.

Mary Alice, who has the distinction of being the first woman to have taught at Yale Divinity School, was initially hesitant to accept the job. She loved her position as the director of children's work for the International Council of Churches, a position she held for sixteen years. She felt her calling was Christian education. At forty-six, Mary Alice's life's work had been in ministry, and she was not sure she wanted to leave it to enter the world of business.

Prior to accepting the job, she shared another concern with Bennet: "I think I can recognize good books for children when I read them, but whether I can select good ideas and secure good manuscripts and see through into books that will sell would remain to be proved. If I should select a succession of duds it would be very hard on both the company and me ... To try out a new field is at once attractive and frightening."

As fate or providence would have it, soon after accepting the job, Mary Alice heard an idea that she thought might make for a wonderful children's book. At a dinner party held in Evanston, Illinois, Mary Alice sat next to a man animated with excitement from traveling to Chincoteague Island, Virginia. The man regaled guests with tales of the Chincoteague Pony swim. He recounted how he "could almost feel the ponies fighting the sea; their nostrils flaring into great round O's to suck in lungsful of air."

Mary Alice peppered him with questions. "Is it a holiday? A pony sale? What is it? And where did the ponies come from in the first place?"

The man elaborated, telling of his experience riding in a boat alongside the feral ponies as cowboys herded them through the salty channel from Assateague Island, to Chincoteague's shore. On Chincoteague, several dozen of the foals would be sold at an auction and go to homes where they would be domesticated. The pony auction proceeds benefited the island's all-volunteer fire department, and the re-homing of colts and fillies would ensure the island herd's numbers were sustainable.

The next day, Mary Alice described the dinner party conversation with Marguerite. The drama of the wild, soaking wet ponies enraptured her. Marguerite determined the only way to find out if the man's tales were as thrilling as he insisted was for her to visit the island Chincoteague for the event called Pony Penning. In 1946, Marguerite traveled from Chicago to Chincoteague, the small island named for the Gingoteague tribe of Indians. Its name translates to "beautiful land across the waters." Assateague, the larger, more easterly island where the ponies live, means "a running stream between."

Marguerite later detailed the genesis of Misty like this: "Just off the shore of Virginia, I heard about a tiny island rising only 21 inches above the sea. Wild ponies lived there, ponies whose ancestors had been tossed ashore from a wrecked Spanish galleon. Here, every July when the ponies were done with feudin' and foalin' the fisherfolk of the island staged a roundup ... the biggest wild west show of the east. And so the little island beckoned, and Misty of Chincoteague was born."

Mary Alice's fears of selecting duds of stories were unfounded. After her death in 1980, Bennet Harvey wrote what appears to be an internal document for Rand McNally: "Mary Alice started writing religious books for Rand McNally & Co. in 1937 and by the mid-1960s, Rand's had sold over 20 million copies of her religious books. In addition to being one of Rand McNally's best-selling authors, she was our Children's Book Editor from 1945-1951 and was responsible for securing outstanding authors, including the one and only best-selling author, Marguerite Henry."

***

"Everyone who yearns to write a book should be fortunate enough to live in Wayne! Source material is just waiting to be mined in every castle and cottage. Experts with the most astounding information are ready to dig up and share the richest nuggets from their past," Marguerite once wrote. Just as Mary Alice's intuition about the Chincoteague ponies making an excellent storybook subject was one factor contributing to Marguerite's author success, so was the community where she lived.

The Henrys had been living in downtown Naperville, most likely in a rental, when they bought what Marguerite referred to as a weathered ranch house in Wayne in 1945. Their new home was located on two acres, a parcel from the original estate of Mark Dunham. He was an importer and breeder of Percheron horses. Dunham built a French-styled Norman castle in the early 1880s, and had stables for five hundred horses on his sprawling seventeen hundred acres.

A 1949 *Publishers Weekly* article described the village where Misty lived for thirteen years as, "a strictly horsey, country-estate community. Almost everyone in Wayne has a horse. The children are put in saddles early and, usually, can curry a pony by the time they learn to comb their own curls." A former resident characterized Wayne as a "mink and manure club."

The Henrys' horse property that Marguerite dubbed Mole Meadow was located only an hour west of Chicago, and even today the village is a world apart from the Windy City. Chicago reverberates with the El's rumble, the cacophony of sports fans and ubiquitous traffic. Wayne's sounds are the cries of birds, and the occasional chugging of a train. In summer, the voice of an echoey horse show announcer peals from

Lamplight Equestrian Center. In autumn, it's the crunch of fallen leaves and a chorus of foxhounds.

Marguerite's helpful and thoroughly horsey neighbors contributed to the authenticity of her books. For example, when she wrote *White Stallion of Lipizza*, her main character was the son of a baker who became a riding master at the Spanish Riding School of Vienna. Wayne resident Susanne Sirotek explained, pronounced and spelled all the Viennese foods the main character would deliver to famous hotels. Susanne also prepared a Viennese dinner for the Henrys.

Marguerite wrote, "I had been so absorbed in the training of the Lipizzaners that I was totally ignorant of the early life of a child brought up on the culinary wonders of Mehlspeisen, Knödels, Strudels, Palatschinken."

Marguerite received letters written in Italian as she penned *The Wildest Horse Race in the World* (first published in 1960 as *Gaudenzia: Pride of the Palio*), the story of the annual Siena, Italy horse races, Katie Lindsay, a joint Master of Foxhounds, "wiser and more fun than any Berlitzer" would translate them. The other joint Master of Foxhounds, George Wood, was Marguerite's next-door neighbor. He and Marguerite chatted over the fence about George Washington's riding skills and foxhunting facts for her title *Cinnabar, the One O'Clock Fox*.

Following the 1961 American Library Association Convention, librarians bombarded Rand McNally with questions about Marguerite's writing methods. They craved a behind-the-scenes look at the author's life. Roy Porter, manager of the Trade Publishing Division of Rand McNally, jaunted off to Mole Meadow to interview Marguerite.

On a hot July day with the air conditioner blasting in her house and a cardinal flitting about in front of the picture window, Roy commented how the panorama of her spacious lawn was an inspiring view for a writer. Marguerite replied, "Well, perhaps, but I work with my back to the window so I won't be distracted by horses and hounds."

I wasn't born yet when Marguerite and her horses lived in Wayne, but thanks to black and white home movie footage I encountered while researching, I've been a guest to Mole Meadow and became acquainted with Marguerite's equine friends.

The fluttering frames open with a shot of Jiggs, the burro she rented from a farmer in Sycamore, Illinois in order to have a muse while writing *Brighty of the Grand Canyon*. The tips of his long ears don't make it into the frame. Marguerite holds a tiger-striped cat up toward Jiggs' muzzle, as if making an introduction, and then places the cat on the burro's back. Jiggs turns his head around to peer at his rider, but is not concerned. In a quick second, Misty is on camera. She nuzzles Jiggs' face, then pins her ears, and shoots him a mare glare. The pony backs her rump toward the burro, threatening to strike. The scene changes and Marguerite's thick-crested Morgan named Friday appears. Marguerite met the black gelding on the sidelines of a polo field in Florida. While vacationing, Sidney spent his days golfing and Marguerite set out for the polo fields. She convinced a trainer to give her riding lessons. She fell in love with Friday and convinced Sidney that Misty was lonely and needed a pasture pal.

The burro grabs the gelding's halter with his teeth and deftly maneuvers under Friday's neck to escape to the other side. In the next scene Marguerite's trio convenes, and Misty bullies Jiggs away from Friday by inserting herself in between the two boys. The celebrity mare insisted on being the center of attention.

I attempted to reach out to the current owner of Mole Meadow. I mailed a letter to their P.O. Box detailing my Marguerite and Misty project. They reached out to me via text initially, and we exchanged a few messages. Then the owner fell silent.

As I connected with current and former Wayne residents, I found out the local historical preservation society receives regular requests from people asking where Mole Meadow is located. People still desire to spot the field where Misty once played. Out of respect for the current homeowner, the location of Mole Meadow is never disclosed. I completely understand wanting to protect privacy, but I can't say I'm not disappointed.

The Dunham Castle still stands today, and across the street a brick red sign with the words "Misty's Meadow" pays tribute to the famous mare who grazed and lazed nearby. The sign is not the exact location where Misty lived, but a rather a three-acre park maintained by the Village. Marguerite and Misty's home is down the road, hidden by mature trees. The barn Marguerite used *Misty* royalties to build, still exists. In the 1980s, a later resident of the ranch house turned Misty's stable into an antique shop. I heard through the grapevine that the current residents were horse people. It was comforting to know Misty's barn no longer housed antiques and had reverted to its proper purpose of housing horses, and I'm glad hooves still thunder down the bridle paths I once traversed on Jim Dandy.

7

FILE FOLDERS, PAPER SCRAPS AND AUTHOR'S CRAFT

"She cared about writing well and she cared for children. I recall her sharing that she 'weeded' adjectives and adverbs from her writing and enhanced the verbs," said Karen Hoyle, the now-retired curator of the Kerlan Collection at the University of Minnesota Libraries, home of the Marguerite Henry Collection. Karen met Marguerite in the 1980s as the university began to steward manuscripts, letters, proofs, photos, and fan mail of the woman whose name has become synonymous with horse books.

Marguerite transitioned easily from writing business and home design magazine articles to children's books. Once she landed on the genre she enjoyed, it was a natural progression to dive into topics that quickened her heart. One child wrote her a letter asking why her books were always about animals and she said, "I feel so comfortable with them. They never complain, never gossip, never go on strike ... Brighty and Misty have become celebrities, but do they want a yacht or a castle? No. A pail of water, a measure of oats, and a loving hand are all they ask. I guess the answer is simple. I like animals."

A journalist once asked Marguerite why she was so driven to write about horses. She explained, "It is exciting to me that no matter how much machinery replaces the horse, the work it can do is still measured in horsepower ... even in the space age. And although a riding horse often weighs half a ton and a big drafter a full ton, either can be led about by a piece of string if he has been wisely trained. This to me is a constant source of wonder and challenge."

I planned a road trip when I discovered that documents from the Kerlan Collection relating to Marguerite were available for exploration—a mere six-hour car ride away in Minneapolis! I'm not a spreadsheet person, but became one when I learned I was allowed to see eight Banker Boxes of archival materials a day. There are thirty-six boxes in the Marguerite Henry Collection. Thirty-six treasure chests filled with clues awaited me. Clues that would add vibrance and texture to the woman I only knew from reading her books and the people I'd met who remembered her from many, many years earlier. I clicked the green Google Sheets icon and titled a spreadsheet "MH Archives," typing *Misty* and *King of the Wind* into the first cell. I plotted out my research adventure.

That first September morning, when I crossed the threshold of the red brick Elmer L. Andersen Library for the first time, I didn't really know what I was doing. I just knew that I would need to wear a mask, sign-in, and place most of my things inside a locker. The library only allowed researchers to use a phone, laptop, pencil and paper while in the reading room. It was understandable. I couldn't remember the last time I used a pencil and didn't think to pack one. Thankfully, my hotel room had a yellow No. 2 pencil with the inscription "We are all still learning," on the desk.

I had two decades of experience guiding sixth and seventh graders to interpret historical documents and artifacts, but that was completely different. In my classroom, I had a teacher's guide to serve as the backbone of the lesson. I also picked up on the energy from the thirty-plus middle school students, mostly eager to learn. Together we pored over photocopied packets reading Hammurabi's Code, examined Martin Luther's 95 Theses, and pondered projected images of the Lascaux cave paintings. This time around I was solo; there was no teacher's guide with suggested answers. This was the real deal. I was about to touch papers that decades earlier had been on the desk of Marguerite Henry. I would hold in my hands manuscripts that she labored over and cherished. My inner history nerd celebrated.

A welcoming librarian trained me on how to page through documents. She demonstrated turning the papers over one at a time and stressed how I should not place them all together in my hand and shuffle them down to get a flush edge. She handed me a manila page, one half of a file folder, labeled "out" as a placeholder to keep track of where to return a file once I'd perused it.

Next, she directed me to the lockers around the corner, where I would "suit up" for research. There, I found a woman who looked like she knew what she was doing, placing her backpack into a locker. I said hello, hoping she could offer me a tip or two on how things worked in a research library. We talked briefly about copyright permissions and informed consent documents. She wished me luck.

When the reading room staff person directed me to "my" library cart filled with Marguerite Henry Collection boxes 2, 15, 18, 19 and 22 stuffed with photos and notes, *Misty* and *Misty's Twilight*, *Album of Horses*, *Justin Morgan* and *Stormy, Misty's Foal*, it occurred to me I had no idea what I was seeking. I just knew that reading documents touched by Marguerite was a privilege, and each one would lead me closer to an understanding of who she was. I hoped that maybe the more I knew about her, the more I could emulate her with my own writing.

I anticipated finding enough behind-the-scenes vignettes relating to Marguerite's life that I could write a handful of blog posts and magazine articles for the equestrian world. I was not sure if there would be enough content for a book, but I wanted there to be. I knew based on an autographed *Misty* book photo I had shared into a Facebook group that amassed over two thousand likes plus in-person conversations with my horse friends, other fans would be delighted to learn more about the real Marguerite. She deserved a book about her life.

What I didn't realize at the time of my first visit to the archives is that with every personal letter I read penned by Marguerite, every rough draft of a manuscript I looked through, each new clue about her life was like uncovering a new layer of what I wanted to do with my life. Here was a woman who built a highly successful career based on what she loved; children, research, writing and horses. Her horse was in her backyard and her husband was a support to her horse craziness. Horses made her happy. Horses make me happy.

Although I will never have the talent of Marguerite, I can apply the lessons I learned from her to my own life. Maybe I could create my own dream job as a Marguerite Henry historian. I had attended a Doris Kearns Goodwin lecture on Abraham Lincoln after she published *Team of Rivals: the Political Genius of Abraham Lincoln*. Doris is a Lincoln historian, and I could be a Henry historian. Although Doris' speech about the sixteenth President was fascinating, her delivery lacked charisma. Granted, I might not be as trained as a historian as Doris, but I knew my public speaking skills were engaging. They had to be in order to keep the wandering minds of my seventh grade students focused during class.

The library was mostly still, with only the occasional sound of another researcher turning a page, punctuating the silence. The first manila file folder I retrieved contained a pile of handwritten notes from the 1940s. I was Nancy Drew. What mystery would I unravel? What would I discover about Marguerite? Was I qualified to conduct the research of a historian? My degree was in political science. Other than writing my master's thesis in education when I became a teacher, I had no scholarly research experience. That was in 1999, literally the last century.

During the first hours of turning over paper after paper, I noticed a pattern: whenever inspiration struck, Marguerite jotted down a phrase. Dozens of manila file folders yielded her writing scrawled on all types of paper. I spied variations of Marguerite's writing: from chicken scratch on random paper shapes and sizes, to the backs of used envelopes, to repurposed backs of mimeographed paper, including one with a list of all her published books up to that point. One note pad with a printed header stating, "The Lord giveth and the IRS taketh away," bears her beautiful, swooping cursive. I smirked at that one.

Besides taking notes and jotting down phrases on whatever paper she had readily available, Marguerite used file folders to strategically organize the research gold she mined—words that would be corralled, then harnessed together, creating pictures for her readers. Her sister Gertrude explained it this way: "I think Marguerite has a unique way of working. Instead of making an outline for her stories she uses a whole riffle of Manila folders, filling them with notes listing what people wore, what they ate, how they lived in the period of her story. The folders are boldly labeled in black crayon and are separated into two groups—those with the plot incidents in their natural progression and those containing background material. One glance at the big black labels gives her a quick visual outline."

For example, in writing *Stormy, Misty's Foal*, Marguerite outlined the story in several folders bearing labels such as "Ponies Huddled," "Misty Evacuated," and "I Feel Blessed; Could have been worse."

Box 22 housed a clipping of the *Salisbury Times* from Monday, March 13, 1962, which detailed the Ash Wednesday storm that killed scores of ponies on Assateague. The word "Rain" is written in black crayon, letters bold with four lines streaming underneath it:

The hard-driven rain slanting under the eaves,
beating on the window pane
At first the rain only plip-plopped
cold bitter rain. Practically snow.

The artful arrangement and word choice stage a drama. Her notes read more like poetry than research. Precipitation morphs from cold plip plopping to sideways rain unleashing violence on the windows. On successive pages, the black crayon continues with more of the story's setting elements. Under "The Wind" Marguerite had written the words "violent winds" beneath "The Sea" along with the descriptors "angry, tide slacking."

The scene for Stormy's birth was drafted with penciled phrases on the back of the draft pages from *The Wildest Horse Race in the World*, her 1960 book featuring the raucous annual horse race held in the city center of Siena, Italy. "Ponies in myrtle bushes in water. Racked up under 'em ... air observers could see about 75 ponies remaining, huddled on high ground." A yellowed, two-paragraph clipping from an unlabeled newspaper was secured onto a yellowed page along with cursive notes directly on the page and then two partial pages—scraps really—of info is glued onto the page. Her writing evolved as mixed media art.

Marguerite's repurposed writing paper wasn't limited to the back of drafts of previous work. I found writing on the back of a piece of cardboard used to keep a new tablecloth in a rigid rectangular shape. I noticed she used the back, blank sides of a stack of 1947 L. Breithaupt Printing Co. calendar pages for notes. Opposite September's orange page, a black crayon heralds "BOWED TENDON" and in blue ink cursive, "a slight protuberance" elaborates on the lameness.

In billowy cursive, phrase after phrase of description, the likes of "sun-dappled roads" and "hills heaped confusedly, one upon another," line two columns, penned on a page awash with setting and description of Vermont's Green Mountains for the book *Justin Morgan had a Horse*, her first horse book. "Lushly green in summer. Kaleidoscope color in fall and a happy combination of snow-white and spruce green in winter."

Marguerite Henry toiled and played with the characterization of place as seriously as that of the people and animals in her books.

Wesley Dennis once wrote, "This ability of Marguerite's to inspire a new reverence for seemingly simple, everyday things is a particular gift of hers for which I am grateful. An old halter, a candle snuffer become more fun to draft after Marguerite has described them."

In a different file, a single-spaced, typed page of notes from the 1939 book, *The History and Romance of the Horse* by Arthur Vernon caught my attention. A black crayon annotation in the margin reads "5 types of nei." I learned through Marguerite, who learned from Vernon, the first neigh is the happy neigh, the second is of desire, the third angry, "issued in sharp, staccato notes." The fourth neigh is one of fear with the words "grave and hoarse" underlined and the fifth neigh is that of sorrow. All these years as a horsewoman I have taken the number of neighs for granted. I would have said there's an angry neigh (commonly heard from a boss mare whose space is invaded) and a happy neigh (which I've only heard my horse do once or twice in the many, many years I've owned him—I'm trying not to take it personally).

The more I immersed myself in the Marguerite Henry papers, the more it dawned on me that she kept files of words and phrases in the same manner I keep files of tax documents and veterinary bills. I remembered reading that as a child Marguerite purchased pushpins with her allowance so she could secure what she referred to as her "precious gems" on her little writer's table in the kitchen. The following quotes adorned her writing space:

> Next to mother's milk, books are the best nourishment.
> — Lawrence Clark Powell

> The more you read, the better you write. — Anonymous

The anonymous quote rang true to me. On the first day of school each year, I asked students to write a letter of introduction to me. I could tell which students were readers by the quality of their writing. Brief letters with tiny sentences lacking in description showed the writer had yet to be entranced by books and had not yet accepted their invitation to adventure or knowledge. One letter I will never forget was several pages. The sixth-grade student confided she had a serious problem: she had already read all the books in her home for her age level, and it was hard to find good books. The young bookworm solved her problem by reading her father's alumni magazines and medical journals. Her dad was an anesthesiologist.

Marguerite, too, continued her bookworm ways into adulthood, even amid a busy writing, speaking, autographing, horse-owning schedule. One file depicted Marguerite's next-level reading habit. A July 1951 apology letter to a local horseman who had agreed to review the Standardbred section from *Album of Horses* reads:

Mr. Dooley Putnam:

I thought you might like to see a copy of the chapter.

So sorry we were late the other night. It was all my fault. My husband and I visited too long at the Baker and then to make matters worse, in driving to Elburn I was reading a book and when I looked up we were in Sycamore.

I smiled at the image of a forty-nine-year-old Marguerite, nose in book, oblivious to the passing cornfields and proximity to her intended destination. Sidney buzzed at least fifteen miles past Flanery Stable where the famed Standardbred trotter Greyhound was enjoying retirement. Marguerite's voracious reading habit from childhood, when she borrowed a new book every other day from the Milwaukee library carried over into adulthood.

Other examples of Marguerite's reading emerge from the Kerlan Collection. She read about writing in an ongoing quest to hone her craft. A newspaper clipping from a 1967 *Chicago Tribune* article about another author is tucked into a file. Marguerite underlined in black marker these lines: "No one in our day—some readers would say no one ever—has written more delightfully about children coping with grownups than has Rumer Godden. Somehow Rumer Godden manages to BE a child when she writes either about or for children. She asks none of the philosophical questions, which adult readers ask themselves. She simply tells what has happened." Marguerite preserved this precious gem after she had already received the Newbery Medal, the highest award for children's literature.

Another clipped article about writing, torn pages from *The Horn Book Magazine,* reveal vertical red marker lines in the margin next to this passage from "The Honest Audience."

"The good children's book is honest, and the reader knows it. It tells a story, and it tells it straight. The boy or girl will not be fooled, and he does not like the book that tries to fool him. He wants to know where he stands. He will accept the most outlandish fantasy if it is made clear that fantasy is intended. He will accept fact if the book is clearly factual. If a writer is confused and confuses him he will have none of the writer or his book."

Marguerite told her stories straight and was not confused. She inspired confidence in us readers to know where we stand in relation to her stories. And just like Rumer Godden, she became a child as she wrote for children, bringing life to stories that stirred our souls.

8

RESEARCHING AND LIVING THE STORY

arguerite delighted in rigorous research and loved libraries. A 1949 *Publisher's Weekly* article said, "Marguerite Henry spends months and months on research work for each of her books. She writes thousands of letters gathering the necessary material. Every detail must be accurate, every statement true, each word the right one with the perfect connotation."

Just how much research she devoted to a subject became evident when I paged through one file titled "Independence Rock" from her papers relating to *San Domingo: Medicine Hat Stallion* while at the University of Minnesota archives. Inside the dossier were two square Kodak snapshots, from two different angles of the granite dome against a pale Wyoming sky. The photos were nestled next to the following:

- 2 stenographers paper's pages worth of notes about Independence Rock

- 18 pages photocopied from a book *Independence Rock: Great Record of the Desert* with images showing names carved into the rock

- 1 page of typed notes taped to the back of a battery company advertisement

- 1 bookmark-sized paper with a sentence about Independence Rock

- 7 copied pages from the aforementioned Independence Rock book with underlines and annotations taped to the back of price lists for Cornell paperboard products

- 2 pages of typed notes about the rock, one observation in black cursive states, "Independence Rock is a low horizontal rock shaped like a French loaf of bread."

- 1 page of photos of Ezra Meeker, the man credited with saving the Oregon Trail

- 1 large copied image of Independence Rock

- 1 poem "Independence Rock" by Addie E. Holmbery of Lader, Wyoming

- 2 pages of notebook paper with a red title of "weather" and "buttes? or mesas"

- 1 description "A big boulder looks like turtle at water's edge," on a scrap of paper

- 1 more page of handwritten notes
- 1 more page of typed description of Independence Rock
- 4 more scraps, bookmark size and smaller of rock description
- 1 postcard of Independence Rock

Marguerite invested hours of research in Independence Rock, the geographic fixture referenced only five times in *San Domingo: Medicine Hat Stallion*. The turtle-shaped boulder makes appearances when Peter, the protagonist Pony Ex rider, dashes past it on his route.

Marguerite traveled over much of the Pony Express route herself, writing to her editor Mary Alice that she took several hundred pictures of "landmarks, way-stations, etc. My desk is heaped high with literally pounds of material. The sifting and sorting is, of course, still going on and will for weeks to come. I like to spend my daytimes on this material, including the books, pamphlets, and articles culled from museums, bookstores and libraries along the way. All of these preliminaries I am enjoying to the full, letting the pieces fall into place before beginning the actual writing."

On my quest to know and become more like Marguerite, I've committed to rigorous research. I spent late night hours scrolling Ancestry.com seeking any shred of detail on her roots. In my eager information gathering, I noticed the house listed as her birthplace on her birth certificate is not the same house listed as her family's home, but the house next door. Was it a misnumbering on the part of the birth certificate scribe or did the doctor who attended her birth live next door? Such a miniscule detail about 794 versus 796 Booth Street in Milwaukee has been just one rabbit trail; the mystery is still unsolved.

Another Ancestry.com discovery that seized my attention was the 1900 Census lists a Breithaupt boy named Lorenz born in 1895. In the next Census—ten years later—he vanished. For months I wondered what happened to him. Did Marguerite have an older brother she never met? Through the research efforts of a downstate Illinois librarian who is passionate about genealogy and happens to own a Chincoteague Pony, I found a death certificate for the brother who died of measles in 1902 at age seven, six weeks after Marguerite was born.

Marguerite researched archival material for her stories, just as I have for her story. I don't remember how I learned that Marguerite published fan newsletters in the 1960s to efficiently answer common questions posed to her in the mountains of fan mail sent from readers around the globe, but the newsletters became my buried treasure. I spent months attempting to track them down via online search engines and on social media with no luck. Finally, one day, during a trip to the St. Charles Public Library, four miles from Marguerite and Misty's Mole Meadow, a librarian handed me a blue folder containing nine photocopied newsletters. I felt like a Triple Crown winner! I hastily scanned every page into an app on my phone so I could read and reread and get to know Marguerite even better through the lost newsletters. When I shared my excitement with the librarian, he said I could check out the folder, just like a book. This worried me. What if some irresponsible library patron made off with this historical prize? Did the librarian even grasp the significance of Marguerite Henry as both a local author and literary giant?

In Newsletter No. 6, written from the Huntington Library in San Marino, California, Marguerite asked, "Would you call it work to have handwritten diaries brought to a private desk of your very own? Diaries written over a hundred years ago? Some are in brownish ink, some in pencil, yet all in such nice and precise script that they are amazingly easy to read. Quite suddenly, you are transported into the past."

Over the course of six days at the Huntington Library, Marguerite read fifty handwritten diaries dated from 1834 to 1875, written by men and women traveling mainly from Pennsylvania, Wisconsin or Illinois to Oregon territory. "It was the intimate details of the people's experiences—their hopes, fears, dangers, tragedies, joys that made them thrilling and important. I felt as if I were an emigrant too, walking alongside the wagon trains, helping to bury the dead, assisting at births, fording or ferrying across streams ... In order to walk in another's boots and in another era it's good to know what his heart and mind are feeling too. That's what I found in those long ago diaries."

Instead of landing in the era of pioneers, my study of Marguerite transported me back in time to the Roaring Twenties of her college years and courtship with Sid. I felt the bright optimism of the 1940s post-war era, and in that moment, sitting with the open file of Independence Rock material of the late 1960s, a few years preceding my birth. I marveled that Marguerite reveled in her time at the Huntington Library, Art Museum and Botanical Gardens, the former estate of the man for whom Huntington Beach, California is named. I've spent many blissful hours there too.

One such outing was a field trip with my middle school students in the early 2000s. I once marveled at the vellum Gutenberg Bible in the museum. Another time, with fellow Anglophile girlfriends, I donned a dress and heels and sipped Earl Grey with cream at the Huntington Rose Garden Tea Room. By myself one February, I drank in the Desert

Garden's winter glory, admiring the sea of aloes, whose pointy plumage gave way to candy corn flowers.

At the Huntington Library, I attended classes on school gardening. My fellow teachers and I became students. We tasted pineapple guavas and learned the easy-to-grow shrub with gray-green leaves and scarlet blooms was both ornamental and edible. We literally played with dirt as we propagated teardrop-shaped Coleus leaves. We created classroom compost bins by drilling holes into Rubbermaid containers, filling them with paper scraps and eggshells so they would later house writhing worms. The goal was to learn school gardening best practices so we could go back to our campuses and facilitate hands-on learning for our students. The kinesthetic experience of letting children plant seeds, water the soil, watch tender green shoots mature and then eat vegetables grown by their own hands would hopefully encourage them to become lifelong earth stewards (and get them excited about eating veggies).

Marguerite was a quintessential hands-on learner. Her curiosity about bluebirds drove her to raise mealworms in laundry tubs in her basement. By observing the "blue forget-me-nots of the air" in her own backyard, she authentically described their habits in *Birds at Home* published by M. A. Donohue and Company in 1942. The idea of a bird book took flight when she and Sidney moved to the country after living their whole lives in big cities. Her interest in identifying birds and understanding the differences between a chickadee and a cardinal and sharing it with children drove the research for the book, her ornithological anthology

While Marguerite found birds intriguing, horses beguiled her. She wanted to learn the distinctions between the breeds: how to differentiate a Belgian from a Clydesdale and a Thoroughbred from an Arabian. Writing a book about horses in a similar format to *Birds at Home* would give her free rein to indulge her curiosity, and that was the genesis of *Album of Horses*. Her enthusiasm for her subject led her to "exciting studies in libraries—borrowing books, ten at a clip and poking around in the stacks for more." After months of library time, she took her research on the road.

"With a bundle of notebooks and a camera, I charged across land and sea—from the Arabian Ranch in Pomona, California, to the Morgan Horse Farm in Vermont: from Thoroughbred and Standardbred stables in Kentucky to the Lipizzaner stud in Austria." She reveled in speaking with all manner of horse people, from the famed Colonel Alois Podhajsky of the Spanish Riding School and Man o' War's owner, Samuel Riddle, to farriers, cowboys and even circus trainers. She claimed the days were never long enough. At night she "bombarded specialists in animal husbandry, genetics, and veterinary medicine" via telephone and letters.

In the Marguerite Henry Collection in Minnesota, I found a 1948 letter to Marguerite from Wayne Dinsmore of the Horse and Mule Association of America. Eighteen equine drawings from Clydesdale to Shetland rim the letterhead. The horses each have a large X through them as though Marguerite were using the letterhead as a visual checklist to ensure she had covered most of the popular breeds.

One merry little research path during the writing of *Album of Horses* became the book *Justin Morgan Had a Horse*. Marguerite could not figure out where to categorize the small horse possessing draft horse strength and racehorse speed. The story of the Morgan's foundation sire, Figure, captured her heart. She wrote his underdog story and brought it to life under the fictional name Little Bub. Marguerite preserved the history of this early American breed, and engaged readers through her historical fiction. Her charging off to the Green Mountains of Vermont has permitted generations of readers to span the centuries and travel by way of the printed page.

Justin Morgan Had a Horse, published in 1945, was the first of several research digressions. *Album of Horses* would have to stand in line for six years behind five other titles before becoming a book.

***

In second and third grade, my best friend Gail and I would go to the Gail Borden Public Library on the banks of the Fox River in Elgin, Illinois and hang out for hours. This was in between playing with our Breyer model horses and cuddling her cats. I was not allowed to have a pet in the house. This made horses even more appealing and to my young mind, practical. A horse is definitely a pet you don't keep in your house. Unless you are Marguerite Henry. She trained Misty to enter the house and allowed her to eat grain off the seat of a chair. The mare was welcome inside to entertain guests and enjoy Thanksgivings and Christmases with her human family.

Both the library's children's room and the larger section for adults beckoned us. From the children's section, we'd locate the cheery yellow hardcovers of Nancy Drew mysteries we had not yet read and the books by Marguerite we didn't own. That's where I met Sea Star, the Chincoteague Pony orphan foal, and Brighty, the burro. In the book room for grownups, we'd linger in the Dewey Decimal areas of 636 animal husbandry/horse care, and section 798, equestrian sports. We had to learn how to groom, tack and sit in a saddle in anticipation for the blessed day we'd become horse owners.

My fellow introvert and I would grab as many delicious books as our thin arms would hold and plop them on the counter to check out. The question, "Will they allow us to take this many books?" flitted through my head, and the good news was that the librarians always checked the books out for us and never even gave us disapproving looks. After amassing our book mountains, Gail and I would retreat to one of our homes and begin reading together independently. My sister Renee, seven years my senior, thought it was weird. Why would you spend time with your friend reading? My thought was then and remains now: Why would you not?

Without the library, horses might not have charged into my life, forever changing who I am and how I see the world. My mom claims I became a skilled reader because of my thirst to know everything about horses. Our second grade teacher Mrs. Valuto held a reading contest. Gail reminded me recently that she and I read over two hundred books a piece. The other kids in our class read fewer than twenty. Those hours spent eagerly reading books for grown-ups about my favorite animal not only imparted knowledge—such as a rider's position in the saddle should allow for a straight line to be drawn through head, shoulder, hip and heel—but unconsciously added new words to my vocabulary.

"My happiest working hours are spent in the library ... there is the miracle of seeing the thin, tangled thread of information which I bring in with me become untangled and laid out in a straight line ... the library is a kind of holy place for me." In the same untitled and undated essay in the archive box with Justin Morgan documents, Marguerite revealed she possessed a "little-girl-at-school feeling" when she was in a library. While she was feverishly taking notes, librarians passed by and helped people, reminding her of friendly teachers. "They believe in me. They charge the whole atmosphere with encouragement and faith."

Another reason Marguerite enjoyed working in libraries was that all around her, other people were "braiding together little strands of information. A serene-faced nun sitting beside me. A rabbi across the table. A pig-tailed youngster reading and daydreaming. Separate entities? No. Somehow we all fit together. We have come to find ourselves ..."

Perhaps library research triggered happy thoughts of childhood. While entering the sacred space of the stacks, fond memories of her first job as a book mender, her time with Miss Ovitz the librarian, and the fresh air as she roller skated to and from the library with a treasure in hand brought back the lightness of youth. Because she felt at home in libraries, it's natural that Marguerite befriended librarians and they gave her story ideas.

Once a story idea grabbed her, Marguerite traveled to the setting and recreated the experiences her historical characters faced. The burro article from *Sunset* that librarian Mildred Lathrop showed her led Marguerite and Sidney to visit the Grand Canyon and descend the North Wall one Valentine's Day morning. The temperature was only five degrees, and Marguerite's fears of the narrow, thirty-inch wide trail were allayed when the trail guide gave her a mailbag filled with letters destined for Phantom Ranch, located on the canyon floor. She reasoned the mail always got through and began enjoying "the splendors of the ride." Meanwhile, Sid was unusually quiet. Marguerite assumed he was too awestruck by the wondrous setting to speak, when in reality he was terrified of heights. This freezing cold ride and additional on-location research yielded the book *Brighty of the Grand Canyon* in 1953. The story centered on a burro who was brave enough to be the first soul to cross the Colorado River suspension bridge, yet gentle enough for children to ride.

Marguerite used immersion journalism techniques, long before the term was coined, by recording and writing with real-life details to capture readers. She once "sampled the burro browse that grew up in sprigs up through rock crevices; I had to know how it would taste," and hiked the trail back up part of the way in order to envision Brighty's ascent. She also camped in the same cave where President Roosevelt, Brighty and Uncle Jimmy Owen (the government lion killer) spent the night.

Beforehand, a park ranger told her if she heard a cry like that of a baby, that would be a mountain lion. "In the dead of night I heard a whimper, followed by cat feet thudding to earth from a blanched tree trunk at the edge of the cave. Terrified, I dived deep into my sleeping bag, like a headless turtle." The next morning Marguerite spotted large paw prints in the wet sand around a pool of water in the cave. That near-cat experience helped her build a scene infused with suspense and danger when Brighty encounters a lion in the chapter titled "The Fight in the Cave."

Another story seed germinated for the 1960 book *The Wildest Horse Race in the World* when Della McGregor, a librarian friend from St. Paul, Minnesota, told Marguerite about the "mystic, mad, wonderful race of the Palio," two summer horse races held annually around the city square in Siena, Italy. Marguerite began saving money for a trip to witness firsthand the Palio and its pageantry, the world's oldest and wildest horse race. Prior to her journey, she spent hours in libraries, gaining as much information about the spectacle as possible. She traveled to Italy three times on research. Two years after beginning her research, she flew to Italy where she lived among the locals to soak up the history and culture of the Palio.

Marguerite did not speak Italian but was skilled in charades and fluent in connecting with people on a heart level. In *Dear Marguerite Henry*, she detailed how she paid a young banker fluent in English to be her translator. "With my interpreter, I talked to the Captain of the Guards, the chief magistrates of the contradas, the official starter of the race, the Palio veterinarian, newspaper editors, professors, and even to His Holiness, Pope John XXIII. Each one gave me a piece of the story until everything fitted neatly into place." While the banker/translator was working, Marguerite struck out on her own with only the simplest of Italian phrases such as hello and thank you. She spoke to locals about the yearly Siena horse race run for neighborhood honor. I can picture Marguerite seated at a long table for a feast surrounded by Siena locals high with the excitement and anticipation of the horse race in the piazza.

During my research in the Marguerite Henry Collection archived in Minneapolis, I encountered a large gray box filled with artifacts from Marguerite's book about Gaudenzia, the gray half-Arabian mare who won Siena's dangerous race three years in a row. I removed the box top and found a typed inventory list. I reached in and examined a sky blue and white jockey's cap that Giorgio, the boy who owned and rode Gaudenzia, wore when he raced for the Onda (wave) district in the Palio. I picked up a faded color photograph of Giorgio, a dark-haired young man wearing khakis, a white dress shirt and serious expression. His smiling parents are seated on concrete steps above him.

I held up an oxhide whip used in the race, and found Italian calendars with images of Palio races and a newspaper article I couldn't read titled, "*La Scrittrice Marguerite Henry e Tornata a Siena dall' Illinois per Conoscere e dire di 'Guadenzia Regina del Palio.'"* The translation meaning: "The writer, Marguerite Henry, came back to Siena, from Illinois, to learn and speak of Guadenzia, Queen of the Palio."

I felt the silkiness of a forest green and orange scarf of *contrada selva* (forest neighborhood), the kind Palio race fans wear to identify their team just as sports team fans wear caps or jerseys with their hometown favorite's logo. I even saw a *spennacchiera*, a horse's headpiece that would be affixed to the racing bridle's browband, shaped like a plump horse show ribbon. In the center of the rosette, a broken mirror shined.

A note on the inventory list said, "This is the actual *spennacchiera* worn in the Palio by Gaudenzia when she won, alone, without a rider, for the contrada Giraffa." Another item on the inventory list said "Correspondence from teacher to whom Marguerite loaned Gaudenzia material for a class project." What a spirit of generosity she possessed!

Collecting these items had a purpose beyond accumulation of mementoes. They inspired and informed her story. Once home with memories of the events, her heart filled with new friendships and a suitcase filled with notes, Marguerite prepared for writing. "I get out a big bulletin board and then I fill it and the desk with all the photographs and other mementoes I've gathered connected with the story and its locale. This helps me to steep myself in the atmosphere of Siena and the Palio or whatever I am writing about—it is like telling the story from my experiences as though I had lived it myself."

The secret sauce of Marguerite's method was relationships with librarians, research on location and creating a space to write with props and photos of the setting. If it worked for Marguerite, maybe it would work for me.

I don't remember where I was or the exact moment it happened. Deep into my research, laughing seagulls and trumpeting stallions swishing through marsh grass called, wooing me to an island off the coast of Virginia. If I was going to emulate Marguerite's methods, a pilgrimage to Chincoteague was in order.

9

STORY FEEDBACK FROM THE SADDLE

"I used to wear a blonde wig and played the part of Maureen Beebe. We would go to schools and libraries with Marguerite and Misty," said Ed Richardson, handing me a plate of cheese and crackers as I stood alongside his kitchen island. It was the summer of 2021.

Fifteen minutes earlier, I was convinced I was lost. I slowed my Jeep down at the edge of a rural road and texted the man Marguerite knew as Eddie. As a little boy, Ed had the enviable opportunity to ride the world's most famous palomino pinto.

I shot off a text, stating I had his address in my GPS app, but I could not see a house. I asked for a landmark. Instead of a landmark, Ed replied with his gate code. I couldn't see his house because the driveway is a mile long.

Once through the gate, a golf course of a lawn and swaths of prairie grasses unfurled before me. Off to the right, a weathered barn with a cupola nestled in a grove of mature trees. I crossed a creek, noticing a wood duck house, and finally arrived, pulling into a circular driveway. I half expected Carson, the butler from Downton Abbey, to come to the door of the stately brick home.

Instead of Carson, a gray-haired gentleman wearing a smile and a blue button-down shirt greeted me along with his wiry-haired, coffee-colored dog. We made our way through the marble foyer and into the kitchen where a letter, a red book about Wayne, Illinois, and a small box were resting on his island.

Marguerite was gregarious and most likely an extrovert. I'm an introvert. I often think of being social and meeting new people as play acting. As much as I was honored to be invited to the home of a stranger who shared history with Marguerite, it was a bit awkward. My actor-self made small talk, commenting on the charming barn on his property I had noticed. I asked if he had horses in it at one time.

Ed explained that the horse barn had been slated for razing as part of a road-widening project near where he grew up. He bought the barn and had it relocated to his property to preserve the over one hundred-year-old structure. He never had horses on this property.

Although Ed rode frequently as a child, even riding to hounds with the Wayne-DuPage Hunt and his family kept horses, he said he never considered himself a horseman. He chuckled, telling me about how the horse he foxhunted would navigate toward low-hanging branches in order to peel him off the saddle.

Three days a week after school, Ed, Tex Drexler (another neighbor boy), and Marguerite would ride together through the same trails I rode thirty years later on Jim Dandy. Ed always rode Misty; Tex rode Jiggs, the burro who inspired Brighty; and Marguerite rode Friday, the former polo pony she brought home from a vacation in Delray Beach, Florida. She persuaded Friday's owner to sell her the black Morgan.

When Ed was around ten and Marguerite fiftyish, she paid Ed seventy-five cents an hour to ride and care for Misty. It was his first job. As they ambled along the country lanes, trails and fields, Marguerite would try out storylines on her riding companions. If Ed and Tex liked her ideas, she would use them. She had her own tiny, trotting focus group.

"So what was Misty like?" I was dying to know, but saved the question until the mid-point of our meeting, attempting to be more sophisticated and less fangirl than I am.

"She was a mean pony."

My heart sank.

But Misty was the stuff of which little girl pony dreams were made! How could I break the hearts of all the Misty fans like me with this revelation?

Ed confessed he got dumped by Misty frequently, and she would try to bite when he'd tighten the girth. The celebrity mare was all mare. Apparently, Misty wasn't the only naughty, yet beloved equine at Mole Meadow. Jiggs would often sit down like a dog, sending Tex sliding to the ground.

Ed told me he never got to ride Friday; Marguerite was the only one who ever rode him.

"Why do you think Marguerite picked you? I would think all the local kids would want to ride the famous pony."

At one of the Misty birthday parties, Marguerite noticed Ed paying special attention to and playing with her Dachshund. Sensing a fellow animal lover, she invited him to be her riding companion.

In fact, Ed loved animals so much he planned to become a veterinarian; however, during his first year in college he contracted mononucleosis and returned home. While recuperating, he helped his dad with his family's fledgling electronics company. Ed never left Richardson Electronics, now a global company. I found out Ed's mom was a teacher at Illinois Park School, the school my dad attended, literally next door to the house where my grandparents lived and he grew up. I later asked my dad if he remembered having Mrs. Richardson as an elementary school teacher, but my dad, then eighty-three, said it was too long ago to remember.

Mid-snacking and chatting, I picked up a photocopied letter from Marguerite. Little Bub, Misty, Sham, Sea Star, Rosalind and Brighty—the main characters from several of her most popular books—gazed back at me from the letterhead. Marguerite's stationery was reminiscent of the letterhead from the Horse and Mule Association of America that I saw at the archives in Minneapolis in the *Album of Horses* box. Was she inspired by that design?

The letter, dated July 14, 1991, written when Marguerite was eighty-nine, started off with an enthusiastic greeting, followed by an apology. "I'm sure you will understand when I tell you the reason for my slow letter-writing is because I'm busy book-writing. Somehow I can't seem to do both at once! <u>Misty's Twilight</u> is my current project, and it's taking shape nicely."

Marguerite shared that the riding adventures with him and Tex "pop into my mind frequently, reminding me of those magical years in Wayne. Writing about Misty's Twilight, a spunky descendant of our Misty, brings those warm memories into sharp focus and tickles my face into a Grandpa Beebe grin, wide and happy." She also told him to give his newborn son a hug from her and to sing *Onward Christian Soldiers* to him when he needed soothing, a hymn the trio of riders would sing together on trail.

She closed the letter with affection, "In my heart you will always be my dear trainer, friend, riding pal and co-singer Eddie. And that's how it shall remain."

"You were very special to her," I said.

"She always treated me like I was an adult, but I was only ten. She was really special."

Ed opened a small box. A pair of bronze button-looking items, about the circumference of a golf ball with the letters "CP," lay next to a small Christmas card. I opened the card.

These were worn by Tony Welling's famous Skippy
(see p. 26 of the Album of Horses).
Merry Christmas,
Marguerite Henry

The CP bridle adornments had anchored the browband of a bay police horse, part of the force in Cleveland, Ohio. Later I re-read "The Morgan" section from *Album of Horses* and had a front-row seat to what could have been a tragic fire in Cleveland, at a circus ground on Lake Erie's shore. In the story, a brave policeman and horse rode into the flames and grabbed the lead rope of the white boss mare. Skippy the Morgan, ponying the herd leader, ushered twenty circus horses out of the smoky mayhem and to safety.

I asked if Rand McNally, her publisher, pushed Marguerite to do all the pony publicity. Ed said no, it was all her. I asked what Sidney was like and Ed said he was a nice man, but he wasn't around that often. As the owner of a dime store in the nearby town of Geneva, Sidney worked many hours.

After a couple of hours hearing Ed's stories, I complimented him on his beautiful cherry tomatoes growing in patio containers. He sent me home with a bagful. Besides the sweet produce, I was grateful for the intimate glimpse into the life of my favorite author.

Over the course of the next year, Ed and I exchanged emails. Whenever I had a question like, "How tall was Marguerite?" (he said she was around 5'7") and "Did you ever meet her sister Gertrude who answered mail for her?" (he didn't), Ed responded rapidly.

We met again, almost a year to the day of our introduction. This time around, he had a scrapbook to show me. A typed invitation to a party hosted by the St. Charles Country Club had an illustration of Misty and Bright Angel, with an announcement bearing a small note in the corner: "Dear Eddie—Don't forget the day. M"

Misty of Chincoteague and Brighty of the Grand Canyon are coming to the Children's Christmas Party. They will put on three playlets with an all-star cast:

Uncle Jimmy Owen played by William Winquist [a local horseman]
Maureen Beebe played by Eddie Richardson
Paul Beebe played by Tex Drexler
Misty, the pony, played by herself

Bright Angel, the burro, played by himself. For each child there will be a Christmas gift in Brighty's pack.

It seems especially appropriate to have Brighty, the burro, with us at this season, for was it not a little long-eared beast that Jesus chose to ride into Jerusalem? Legend says Jesus wanted to reward his patient burden bearer, so he marked him with the emblem of the cross. And ever since, the burro has worn a dark stripe down his back and withers over his shoulders for all the world like the symbol of the cross.

If your children would like to trace their fingers along Brighty's cross and gaze into his wistful eyes, he will stand very still, returning the adoration in full measure.

A large Santa Claus with a text bubble announcing, "I'll be here too!" seemed to be an afterthought. What a party that must have been.

"Did neighbors think Marguerite was eccentric, bringing Misty into the house and having parties with a pony?"

"No. Everyone loved her." That seemed to be an emerging theme.

I also wanted to know how a pony Ed deemed as mean would allow throngs of fans to press in to be near her. I had seen photos of swarms of children clamoring to touch her. How would Misty tolerate all the kids, commotion and crowds, but not kick or bite?

I posed the question.

"Misty would do anything for Marguerite," Ed said.

Just like a mare.

***

As eager as Marguerite was to have children weigh in on her storylines, she was equally enthusiastic about fact checking. In one archival letter from 1976, Marguerite wrote to a man from the Chincoteague Volunteer Fire Company seeking help recalling details about the *Misty* movie premiere in 1961. Marguerite was in the middle of writing the book *A Pictorial Life Story of Misty*, and needed help reconstructing the events from fifteen years earlier. I read the letter almost fifty years after it was sent.

Her letter began, "Readers love cozy details so they can picture a scene as if they were right there." Like a teacher assigning homework, Marguerite included six pages, each with two or three questions at the top of the page, followed by ample blank space to fill in a hand-written response.

One page starts like this: "I remember Miss Victoria Pruitt helping to raise money to buy uniforms for the High School Band. I'd appreciate knowing the colors of the uniforms in 1961. Would the band have played some special numbers?"

Part of why Marguerite requested these event details was due to the passing of time, but in a PostScript, she reveals a distracting and dangerous experience that explained why the band's presence was far from mind. The P.S. declared, "I remember the parade vividly—BUT FROM ONE ANGLE ONLY." She recalled Misty leading the lineup, hand walked by Uncle Ralph Beebe, followed by a stallion named Silver King, hitched to a pony cart.

"Wesley Dennis and I were in the cart, Wes driving. Silver King may have been gentle to ride, but I don't think he'd ever been driven before. He took off at a gallop for Misty. His check strap broke, and he tried to kick the cart to kingdom come. Fortunately, a roundup man on the sidelines had a piece of thong [leather] in his pocket. He stopped the pony, Wesley repaired the check strap, and we took off again, both of us feeling that at any moment the strap would break again. The spectators were laughing hilariously, and Wes and I were laughing hysterically. Now you know why I don't remember much about the parade. I was too busy hanging on!"

In the era before computers, search engines and email communication, writing, mailing and waiting for return correspondence would demand a large time commitment and patience. I thought back to my time with Ed Richardson. I asked if he recalled Marguerite having hobbies. He said she was always working, and books were all over her house.

During her writing process, Marguerite hand wrote all her books. She once stated she felt happier with a pencil in her hand as "it is almost like caressing the words." Marguerite then paid a typist to take her cursive manuscript to typeface. Once the manuscript was typed, she would give the story to Sidney, and observe his reactions. If his brows knit together, she knew that was a part of the story she would need to further finesse. When she saw him shed a tear, she knew that passage was a victory. When Marguerite released a new book, Sidney reportedly had a copy bound with a leather cover, making it a one-of-a-kind edition.

I wish I knew the whereabouts of Marguerite's special collection of leather-bound books.

10

THE STRUGGLE OF BRIDLING PEGASUS

I'll never forget sitting on the back porch of my family's yellow house, cardboard-covered book in hand, as my older sister Renee read how the little boy in *The Carrot Seed* walked off with the world's largest carrot. The carrot was imposing, bigger than the boy. It was so huge it had to be carted away in a wheelbarrow. This was after the family naysayers—dad, mom and big brother—all told the little boy his seed he planted and diligently watered and weeded, "won't come up." Thanks to Renee's reading the book to me on repeat, one day the words leaped out at me. I recognized them and was speaking them aloud to her while following along on each page. On that blessed day in the early 1970s, I could read!

Once I began reading, I never stopped.

Renee wasn't my only family reader. My mom sat at the edge of my bed and read *The Bible in Pictures for Little Eyes* to me every night before she tucked me in. I can still see the cover illustration of a baby Moses in his basket at the edge of the Nile River being discovered by Pharaoh's daughter. At some point, I discovered writing and illustrating stories, both alone and with my library friend Gail. She penned an illustrated series about a friendly purple monster named Plum. My stories featured a girl named Joan, and the horses dancing their way into my narratives were always spirited Arabians.

It would seem a celebrated author such as Marguerite Henry possessed a natural talent for word play straight from the womb. In my teacher credentialing program, I learned parents who are readers will generally instill both the skills and value in their children. Also, older siblings' reading promotes literacy in younger siblings. This grad school fact played out in my classroom experience in two vastly different schools: one was an affluent Los Angeles middle school, while the other was an under-resourced charter school in Chicago. Marguerite's father was in the printing profession and her mother, a housewife, was a reader of women's magazines. Being the youngest was another factor that undoubtedly spawned her skill with words.

As much as Marguerite loved writing, and it came naturally to her, she confessed in unpublished notes for the anthology *Something About the Author*, written when she was eighty-six years young, "My writing life wasn't always easy. There were apprentice years when I wrote 16 geography books, each one took at least six weeks and was paid $25 per book. My cleaning lady at that time earned the same amount once a week working from 8 to 1, although I'll have to admit my work was more fun."

Marguerite compared writing a book to pregnancy. When asked how long it took for her to write a book, she said it took as long as a mare to carry a foal—eleven months. When her publisher asked if she was sure she really wanted to write *King of the Wind*, a book where the main character was a boy who can't speak and the supporting characters were a horse and a cat, also mute, she responded she was pregnant with the story.

A fan named Brian once wrote asking, "Is it hard to be an author, or is it fun? I would like to know this because I am writing my first book."

Marguerite replied, in Newsletter No. 4, "Dear Brian, It is both. Some days when your characters behave and everything goes right, you wouldn't change places with anyone in the world. But there are days when you tear up most of what you write. Even then, you know you couldn't be happy doing anything else."

In a 1961 speech delivered at the Children's Book Fair Luncheon Preview titled "Who Carry Umbrellas," Marguerite revealed one writing assignment early in her career was nearly her last. For months she labored over the piece, ultimately taking too much time finishing it due to "interruptions, interruptions, interruptions." The day she submitted the work to her editor, *The Saturday Evening Post* scooped her story. Nevertheless, she persevered, just like the little boy in *The Carrot Seed*.

In the speech, Marguerite delineates how her failure motivated her to learn best practices for writing. "In white fury I sat down at my typewriter and banged out letters to big name writers who were not scooped ... How, I asked them, do you find peace and quiet? How do you escape the little gnatlike interruptions that pick away at time and thought? What are your work methods? In short, how do you bridle Pegasus?" She mailed twenty letters asking for advice to Eleanor Roosevelt, George Bernard Shaw, Thornton Wilder and Somerset Maugham, to name a few. All the literary luminaries wrote Marguerite back.

As I pored over the advice gleaned from her correspondence, I realized the collective wisdom from the early Twentieth Century is still relevant, perhaps even more so in this age of short attention spans, pervasive technology, and social media platforms. I battle with writing and ignoring distractions every day. Instagram notifications and an email stream pique my curiosity when I attempt to have a single focus of stringing words together. A desire to make a Nespresso, text my friend, watch a funny video, or check out the latest group message in WhatsApp pull me away from my paragraphs.

It's nice knowing I'm not alone; Marguerite struggled with distraction too.

Irish playwright George Bernard Shaw replied to Marguerite's letter asking for his advice with the following: "I began my literary career without the means to choose my surroundings. I had either to write under all circumstances or not to write at all."

Shaw, who penned *Pygmalion*, the inspiration for the beloved musical *My Fair Lady*, and later *Saint Joan*, a play that garnered him the 1925 Nobel Prize for Literature disclosed, "A very considerable part of my plays were written while on railway carriages between King's Cross and Hatfield; and it is no worse than what I have written in the Suez and Panama Canal."

Marguerite didn't write from the Suez or Panama canals, but once from a fire hydrant, another time from a department store glove counter and even in a dressing room. One of the most amusing accounts from her magazine writing was the time when she was in New York City and had an interview with William H. Ingersoll, a partner in the company that created the first $1 pocket watch. Marguerite described him a a man "whose mind is a machine gun of ideas."

At the conclusion of their interview, Marguerite stated she was "all adither." There was not a good spot for her to jot down Ingersoll's insights. Undaunted, she flew into a women's dressing room at Saks Fifth Avenue, only to discover that she didn't have her notebook. "Hastily I grabbed a handful of paper towels and began scribbling feverishly, filling sheaf and sheaf of paper with Mr. Ingersoll's very words. A week later when I returned home, I confidently took the sheaf of towels out of my bag. What consternation upon preparing to write the story to find that all of the writing had disappeared!"

From Thornton Wilder's letter, Marguerite learned another trick of the trade. The author of *Our Town,* and a three-time Pulitzer Prize-winner wrote, "When you are held up in plot or character development, get out and take a walk. Stride and tramp out your material." He also shared a Gertrude Stein quote: "It takes lots of loafing to write a book."

In her speech, Marguerite told the luncheon audience that she didn't stride out the material, but she had another strategy. "I climb aboard my black horse Friday and trot and gallop it out. Occasionally, we meet up with screaming fire trucks or huge mechanized corn pickers. Then Friday bolts and flees while I hang on for dear life, prayerfully, breathlessly singing, 'Jesus loves me, this I know.'"

After those exhilarating rides, her mind would become clear. "The hurdle which blocked my progress miraculously, almost mysteriously, disappears." I too find a way through my out-of-the-saddle problems on horseback. My horse Knight is not a spooker, thankfully.

Perhaps the most matter-of-fact advice gleaned from her letter-writing campaign to other writers came from Howard Vincent O'Brien, a journalist for *The Chicago Daily News*. "This peace and quiet business is mostly nonsense. It is an evasion practiced not by people who write, but by people who would love to have written."

Marguerite disliked peace and quiet. She claimed she was unable to write alone. Those days at her tiny desk in her mother's kitchen in Milwaukee perhaps shaped her concept of the ideal writing environment. She liked the feeling of others around her also working.

As an adult at Mole Meadow, her Dachshund Alex was her writing companion, working alongside her. "His self-appointed task is with the wastebasket." The dog would remove pages that had been disposed of one at a time, which he then tore "into infinitesimal bits, so that I can never be tempted to retrieve a discarded phrase." If Sidney ran errands with the dog, Marguerite would "dash off to a library" so as to not work in solitude.

The years Misty lived with her, Marguerite wrote from 8 a.m. until 1 p.m., then went outside to be with her horses. In a 1979 interview with the *Los Angeles Times* Marguerite said she wrote five hours a day longhand, a practice she committed to throughout her career. In *Dear Marguerite Henry*, originally published as *Dear Readers and Riders*, a Dear Abby-esque exchange of letters from children, she divulged she loved the German poet Goethe's advice. "Use the day before the day. Early morning hours have gold in their mouth."

Another writing challenge Marguerite grappled with was golf, or actually engaging in a lengthy social and sporting activity that was not writing or riding. Sidney's passion for golf meant taking regular winter golf holidays. In a 1966 or 1967 letter to Bob Brislawn, a cowboy source for her book *San Domingo: Medicine Hat Stallion*, Marguerite shared that another couple from Wayne joined the Henrys for their sunny golf getaway. The wife was an avid golfer who insisted Marguerite played every day. "I felt as frustrated as a horse on the wrong side of the fence because 18 holes on a very difficult course laced with water hazards and gouged with sand traps is sheer torture for me. I took two or three strokes to everybody's one."

There was an Arabian horse ranch an hour from where they were golfing with a mare who had just given birth to two healthy twin foals. "Every time I dubbed my shot, I yearned to do a story about those twins, but I never even saw them!"

Marguerite showed tenacity up until the last days of her life. *Misty's Twilight*, a book about a remarkable great-great grand foal of Misty published in 1992, was written in first person. The publisher asked Marguerite to change the point of view to third person. She rewrote it. She was nintey.

Marguerite, who yearned to be an expert at her craft since girlhood, had learned to bridle Pegasus. We readers, writers, and horse lovers are the beneficiaries.

11

THE PINNACLE OF SUCCESS

There was one box I could not wait to get my hands on while researching Marguerite's personal papers in the Kerlan Collection in Minneapolis: Box 29. It did not contain the Holy Grail, but to me, it might as well have been. The box held Marguerite's Newbery Medal for *King of the Wind*, her story about Sham, the underdog Arabian who became a founding sire of the Thoroughbred. It won the John Newbery Award in 1949. *Justin Morgan Had a Horse*, Marguerite's first horse book, and *Misty of Chincoteague* won Newbery Honors as runners up in 1946 and 1948 respectively. The third time was a charm for the dauntless author, who won the most prestigious award for children's literature with her twenty-ninth published book.

The research room of the Anderson Library was silent. My brain was loud with thoughts as I stood up from the chair and peered into the

Bankers Box to locate the folder housing the medal. *Will it look like an Olympic medal? What is the design? What did this award mean to Marguerite?*

My first exposure to Newbery winners was via teachers reading them aloud to my classes when I was in pigtails. I listened intently to *Johnny Tremain* and *From the Mixed-up Files of Mrs. Basil E. Frankweiler*, the 1944 and 1968 awardees. I don't remember which teachers read them, and the storylines are now hazy, but I knew the Newbery books were special and worth reading. Being able to see and hold in my hands such a distinguished prize was going to be a thrill I would long carry with me.

The Newbery Award, named after John Newbery, a British bookseller credited as the first to publish a children's book, was launched in 1922 by *Publisher's Weekly* editor Frederic Melcher. The award had three goals: "To encourage original creative work in the field of books for children. To emphasize to the public that contributions to the literature for children deserve similar recognition to poetry, plays, or novels. To give those librarians, who make it their life work to serve children's reading interests, an opportunity to encourage good writing in the field."

Melcher underwrote the Newbery Medals for decades, prizes cast in bronze by René Paul Chambellan, a sculptor whose works are seen today in Rockefeller Plaza's fountain and the Art Deco grand entrance of the Chicago Tribune Tower.

When I picked up *King of the Wind* as a girl, it was for my own pleasure. I dove in not for the literary merit, but for the horses. I don't think I even realized it was a Newbery winner. While immersed in its pages, I was swept away across centuries. I journeyed with Agba, the mute stable boy who saved the sultan's orphan foal with love and camel's milk. When Sham matured into a stunning stallion and was gifted to

King Louis XV of France, I imagined voyaging across the Mediterranean with the boy and horse.

My spirit drooped when Sham emerged from the ship so undernourished, he was deemed unworthy of royal life and sold as a cart horse. I felt like I was there every step of the way as the horse and his devoted friend endured hardship, separation, reunion, exile, then redemption. It was satisfying to me as a reader when Sham's worth was finally recognized and his greatness heralded by the King and Queen of England.

The Newbery Medal rested in a black felt frame about the size of a square coaster. I slid the award out onto the table from a box the size of a checkbook bearing a photocopied image of the medal taped to its lid. One side of the medal read, "For the most distinguished contribution to American literature for children." Marguerite's name and the year are engraved onto an open book with a torch blazing behind it and a laurel wreath encircling it like a horseshoe. The opposite side of the medal depicts a mustached gentleman in a formal suit, presumably John Newbery, holding a book. The man is flanked by a boy in knickers and a seated girl, both with arms outstretched, desiring to hold the book.

Like an excited paparazzo, I snapped several photos of the medal. I shot the front side and the back side, then placed my pencil and eyeglasses next to the medallion for scale. I immediately texted the photo to my mom and a few friends.

Long before I took the class Multicultural Education, on the lengthy and rigorous path to becoming a teacher, Marguerite Henry introduced me to people from other cultures in *King of the Wind*. I didn't understand the Ramadan fasting or the call to prayer in the opening scene of the story, but I understood Agba's devotion to a horse. The boy on the other side of the world living in another era who practiced a different religion wasn't so different from me. Marguerite fostered my love of horses and simultaneously opened my eyes to the world beyond my small-town neighborhood. Over the years, I realized excellent literature instructs without lecturing and entertains while sparking questions. Marguerite wasn't my only author/teacher.

Before I held Marguerite's Newbery award, I had seen gilded stickers of the medal adorning books on my apple red shelves in Room 31, my classroom for twenty years. My students and I read and loved the 2000 Newbery winner, *Bud, Not Buddy*. Bud ran away from an orphanage to find his dad, a big band musician. The little boy made us both laugh and reflect as he indirectly taught us about the Great Depression and segregation.

We cheered for Meg in the 1963 Newbery winner, *A Wrinkle in Time*, as the brilliant teen with low self-confidence who, despite her foibles, saved her father from Camazotz, a planet of conformity.

We admired *Maniac Magee*, the fleet and unassuming orphan teen in the 1991 Newbery winner who could untangle any knot, no matter how challenging, and befriended both sides of a racially divided town. Newbery Medal books are not just for children.

I wondered how *King of the Wind* came to life and pieced together clues revealing its origin. It started when Walter Chrysler, the automobile magnate and Thoroughbred breeder, commissioned Wesley Dennis to draw the head of the Godolphin Arabian on his personal stationery. The illustrator hired a cousin as an assistant to search out artists' likenesses of the stallion born in 1724. As she dug into the research, it wasn't the thick-crested horse's image that intrigued her, but his underdog story. She decided to write a biography of the stallion, and Wesley was eager to illustrate it.

While collaborating with Marguerite on *Justin Morgan Had a Horse*, Wesley hinted at this historical horse story he knew would make for an outstanding book. Marguerite implored him not to tell her more. "I can't trust myself to know about it if someone else is at work on the idea." Years passed and Wesley's cousin never got around to writing the book. After negotiating with the cousin, Marguerite was free to tell the story of Sham, the swift steed with a wheat ear cowlick on his chest.

Once the *King of the Wind* origin story materialized, curiosity drove me to learn how the Newbery Medal winner is determined. I found archival material relating to Marguerite's win, and even discovered a woman who played a role in selecting the Newbery Medal and Honor winners from the early 2000s.

Twenty-one Newbery-Caldecott Committee members, a selection team composed of librarians and educators, selected *King of the Wind*. It won "by a striking majority." Retired University of Minnesota professor Lee Galda was on the 2003 committee that selected the winner, *Crispin: the Cross of Lead* by Avi, and she pulled back the curtain on her experience.

"It was a year of reading and it was just wonderful. You couldn't see the floor because of all the books. You read, rank and narrow down. A huge pile of books is in contention at the American Library Association meeting and you sit around the table taking turns and don't interrupt and listen to what people have to say. You vote then do it again and vote again. It keeps on going until it goes down to a handful. The selection process lasted two days."

Winning the highest prize for children's literature is the pinnacle of success for an author. In addition to acclaim and media coverage, the

Newbery Medal translates into endorsements from librarians and teachers, leading to increased book sales.

Following Marguerite's win, Frederic Melcher held a press conference in New York City to announce the winners and hosted a luncheon. Despite a blustery snowstorm, reporters and photographers came out in force. Wesley Dennis was a surprise guest as his illustrations contributed so much to the story. Elmer and Berta Hader were also there, the husband-and-wife team who won the Caldecott Medal, which Melcher instituted in 1937, for their picture book *The Big Snow*.

In the wake of the award announcement, *Publisher's Weekly* reported, "The more you know about the author of the prize-winning book, *King of the Wind* (Rand McNally), the more certain you become that no accolade has ever been more judiciously presented. You'll never learn from Marguerite herself about this highest of honors in the juvenile field that she has won. Would that the great in all avenues of creative accomplishment were as modest as Marguerite Henry!"

Mary Alice Jones, the editor who worked alongside Marguerite on *King of the Wind* further emphasized Marguerite's modesty in a statement after the big win, "It is a delight to work with her on a manuscript. She is so eager for suggestions, so delighted with the smallest contribution in the way of an idea or phrase that she makes one feel her own joy in creating the material. And when it's finally completed and published and offered to the public, she seems to have a continual feeling of surprised pleasure that people really like it well enough to buy it."

People didn't just like *King of the Wind*, they loved it. And the Newbery Medal led to a flurry of invitations to schools, book fairs, horse shows and libraries, not just for Marguerite, but for Misty also. According to Marguerite, "One day the world in all its bigness opened out for Misty with a formal invitation to her from the American Library Association." Author and pony were invited to the American Library Association convention in Grand Rapids, Michigan, which was about to host twelve hundred attendees. A stall was prepared for Misty in the auditorium exhibit hall and plans were made for an appearance at the local department store Herpolsheimer's.

Eddie Pacuinas, the horseman who trained Misty to be a riding horse, trailered the pony two hundred miles to the ALA conference. Once in the host city, a braided and halterless Misty attended an early morning meeting of librarians clad in skirt suits and scarves. A photo in *A Pictorial Life Story of Misty* shows the mare in a cluster of women seated in rows. Misty's muzzle is at Marguerite's shoulder. A straight-faced woman in a feathered hat sits directly behind the pony's hindquarters while a woman wearing a horse pin on her lapel grins.

According to Marguerite, the pony took her exercise on city streets where her shoes made a ringing sound she'd never heard before. At 5 p.m. she leaped into the hotel elevator and traveled to the seventh floor where she hobnobbed with the president and vice president of Rand McNally and the director of libraries for the Chicago Board of Education. The dignitaries gave her carrots. "They all talked to her in low conversational tones to make her feel at ease." Of all the important people, Marguerite wrote Misty knew no one but they all knew her.

Four hundred and ninety-eight attendees paid $4.50 a plate for dinner to witness the Newbery-Caldecott award ceremony and hear the speeches of both Marguerite and Elmer Hader. Guests found two mementos at their place setting. A small metal horse, mane and tail held high as it galloped, was a nod to Sham, and a white and gold decorative snowball for *The Big Snow*.

Misty stood in her temporary stall at the Rand McNally booth of the Hotel Pantlind. She was not allowed to attend the banquet. Marguerite began her acceptance speech, "King of the Wind was a long time growing. At first it was nothing but a letterhead. A letterhead and a wish." Marguerite shared the genesis and evolution of the project with the eager audience.

Marguerite concluded her speech, "Sometimes a book gives you a small moment of happiness; and sometimes when you close the cover, the book grows big within you, like a boll of cotton bursting its seams ... if it weren't for deadlines I'd still be working on *King of the Wind*. The doing is always so much more fun than the getting through ... Now this book is finished. Sham has been crowned, and in the crowning Agba too has been honored. As custodian for them I accept the Newbery Medal."

After the ceremony, Misty visited the banquet hall to have her photo taken by *The Grand Rapids Press*. She stood in front of the head table, between the long rows of tables, with linen napkins askew, ashtrays filled, and chairs pulled out at different angles. Pinned to a braid, Misty wore a horseshoe-shaped corsage of roses.

Misty's appearance at the literary event of the year received mixed reviews. In a letter from Virginia Chase, president of Children's Library Association to Helen Kinsey of the ALA, Chase wrote, "In case you wondered if CLA had lost its wits by having Misty there, you will be interested to know that the CLA Board to the last man decidedly voted against the horse and was assured by Headquarters that she would not appear ... I hope no one else at Headquarters thinks we wanted the horse or even lifted a finger to get her there."

In a response, Helen Kinsey wrote, "I would say that Misty was a huge success, enjoyed by everyone ... even Mr. Cory remarked on what

Misty's attendance meant in the way of publicity for both ALA and Grand Rapids Public Library."

She might not have been welcome with a segment of the library world's leaders, but she received a warm welcome at an autograph party the day after the banquet at Herpolsheimer's department store. Book display counters were removed "to provide space for a stall for Marguerite Henry's little island horse, Misty, which proved, over a two-hour period, to be a perfect guest." During the pony party Marguerite signed books by the hundreds and Misty delighted "hordes of children who crowded the store."

When I somehow discovered the transcript of Marguerite's Newbery acceptance speech, as well as an article written by her sister Gertrude, titled "My Little Sister Marguerite Henry," were published in the 1950 January-February issue of *The Horn Book Magazine*, I scoured online shopping sites to locate a copy. It was gratifying to procure the antique magazine, and even more so when it arrived in my mailbox. To my delight, the cover art featured a scene of three huntsmen blowing their hunting horns atop a chestnut, bay and dapple gray. When I turned to page 2, the letters to the editor section was titled "The Hunt Breakfast," with the explanation "In this section of each issue you will find such informal comment on books, authors, magazines and the book world generally as would take place at a breakfast of a Hunt Club for which The Horn Book Editors were MFHs [Masters of Foxhounds]."

In her tribute, Gertrude proudly listed all the literary awards Marguerite had received by that point. "Three of her books had been Junior Literary Guild selections: *The Little Fellow*, *Justin Morgan Had a Horse*, and *Misty of Chincoteague*. *Justin Morgan* received the 'Friends of Literature' Award for 1946. *Benjamin West and His Cat, Grimalkin* was listed by the Library of Congress among juvenile books of 1947 best expressing the American spirit. It has been translated into two foreign languages and done into Braille, as has also *King of the Wind*. *The Little Fellow* has just gone into a Spanish edition."

She then wrote, "Just as highly treasured as these recognitions, however, are the letters which come to Marguerite Henry from boys and girls. Honors and awards are sobering almost frightening to her, and there is little danger that they will ever go to her head; but in my case there is now more than ever a driving urge to dash out of the house as I did upon Marguerite's birth, and boast to all the neighborhood about my little sister!"

Gertrude's article includes a preschool-age looking Marguerite, in button up boots, tights, cotton dress and a large white bow pulling back her little girl bob. Another photo shows the two word-loving sisters as little girls standing on the step of their front porch in Milwaukee. Yet another photo depicts Marguerite, swamped by fans, at a book signing. A final pair of pictures shows two upper elementary school-age boys that the article states, "will bicycle eight miles to her [Marguerite's] house for the 'privilege' of cleaning the stable and currying Misty..."

In one photo, the Misty fans sit in front of the pony's white Dutch door as Marguerite and Misty peek out above. The other photo has Misty with her left front leg on the stool and Marguerite holding her right cannon bone in a shake. One boy stands at Misty's side with his hand on her barrel. The caption reads, "Richard Beltz pointing to the map on Misty's withers."

As fate or destiny would have it, my mother had bragged to a golf friend about my Marguerite project. The friend told my mom, "My husband used to ride his bike from Elgin to Wayne to go see Misty."

Although her husband had passed away, my mom's friend provided her with a sticky note bearing the name and address of her husband's bike-riding companion. I eagerly composed a letter to Richard Beltz, who long ago befriended Marguerite, and mailed it with a heart full of hope.

One November day, as I sat in a coffee shop sipping a honey latte laboring over this chapter, my cell phone illuminated with the name Richard Beltz!

12

FAN MAIL AND FRIENDSHIP

Over the course of writing this book, I have composed and mailed letters to several people who knew Marguerite or had a connection to her. None of the letters have reappeared in my mailbox stamped "return to sender," but only a few have received replies. I was disappointed that my missive mailed to Leif Garrett, the former teen idol who played Peter in the 1977 movie *Peter Lundy and the Medicine Hat Stallion* based on Marguerite's book, never got a response. I thought my odds of hearing from him were good, since I couldn't imagine the former *Tiger Beat* cover boy and *Celebrity Rehab* reality show star was inundated by fan mail today.

As my fingers hovered over my laptop keyboard in the coffee shop, I was surprised to see Richard Beltz's name on my phone screen.

My brain was not in interview mode but I answered with a hello and a smile, quickly opening a new Google doc in order to type my way through my conversation with Richard. I thanked him for calling me, and he said he was interested in my return address because his grandfather had owned two farms in the town where I live. He recalled his grandfather driving a 1938 Oldsmobile into town to sell chicken eggs to the market. Richard called me from his "couple hundred acre" ranch in Wyoming that has been in his wife's family since 1909. I commented that it was impressive (having a ranch). He said his place was small, and his neighbor's ranch was seventy thousand acres.

Richard met Marguerite in 1949. His teacher introduced him to the book *King of the Wind*, mentioning the woman who wrote the story was a local author. Somehow Richard, eleven at the time, found Marguerite and Mole Meadow. He and his buddy, visited Marguerite, then forty-seven, three to four times a week that summer.

Richard pedaled his red Monarch alongside his friend Denny for about an hour on a mostly flat country road. He would help Marguerite by cleaning her yard or brushing Misty and Friday the Morgan. Marguerite would make her young friends and helpers bologna or peanut butter and jelly sandwiches.

"That was definitely a different era. I can't imagine parents today letting a kid ride their bike eight miles along a road unsupervised," I observed. Let alone hang out for the day with someone who was technically a stranger, I thought, but didn't say.

Richard served twenty-one years in the Air Force doing heavy ground radar industrial safety compliance in Colorado Springs. When he retired he worked at the Air Force Exchange Commissary. Richard doesn't travel much these days, but sees mountain lions, deer, and occasionally, moose on his ranch. After our conversation, I made a copy of the magazine article of Marguerite, Misty and Richard and mailed it to him.

It turns out Richard and I weren't the only readers who desired a more personal connection with Marguerite. Forty file folders filling three Bankers Boxes of the University of Minnesota's Marguerite Henry archival collection contain fan mail and photographs. The days I spent in the research room, I dug into folder after folder, reading fan mail, on a mission to uncover the woman behind the beloved books. The notes and letters did not disappoint.

Alice Crowson sent a letter to Marguerite in 1979. "What I like is that you don't make the story boring by writing 'horse ran over the river, through the valley, across the plain (yawn).' Your books are exciting, full of life and fun and parts that make you laugh and some that make you cry, beautiful, wonderful parts that fill you with a precise picture of the scene and they always leave you feeling warm and like you know the person (or horse.)"

One heartfelt run-on sentence illustrated Crowson's enthusiasm for Marguerite's tales. What might have made Alice's English teacher cringe most certainly warmed Marguerite's heart.

I feel the same way, Alice!

Another letter blew my mind with a story of family togetherness, thanks to Misty. An eighteen-year-old big sister wrote, "Remember me? I've written to you before." (A number of letters contained "remember me?" showing Marguerite had repeat correspondence with some fans.) The letter writer's horse crazy younger step-sister received a copy of *Misty* along with the Breyer model of the pony for Christmas. The older sister had been to Chincoteague and had met the real Misty. The younger sister, a sixth grader, grabbed the Misty book and urged her big sister to read it to her. "I was so enthusiastic about it I couldn't stop reading and they wouldn't let me. My stepmother and even my father sat down to listen until I had finished the book. I read the whole book in one day and enjoyed every minute of it," the teen shared with Marguerite.

I loved the picture of unity this letter represented and wondered if such a scenario could even occur today with ubiquitous cell phones and social media. The image of the pleading little sister and the willing older sister immersed in sea air, shaggy-maned ponies and the rhythms of the tide, turning page after page in delight was so magnetizing the parents joined in.

The other aspect that struck me as unusual was that a sixth grader would have the reading skills to navigate *Misty* on her own, yet she craved sharing the story with her sister who had seen the palomino pinto in person. Maybe she inherently knew that the words on the page would come alive in a special way only possible by a reader/narrator who had lived a Chincoteague experience. Whatever the reason, the family's impromptu story time via Misty gratified me as a teacher.

Most of the letters I perused had the abbreviation "ans." in cursive in an upper margin. Replying to fan mail was of supreme importance to Marguerite—so much so that while she was traveling, her sister Gertrude would reply to fan mail on her behalf. Marguerite was quoted in a newspaper article as saying she believed each letter from a child was a sacred trust. Children trusted her so much they wrote her asking advice as though she were a horsey Dear Abby.

In the late 1960s, at the suggestion of her editor, Marguerite launched a newsletter to connect with fans and reply to their most commonly asked questions. The debut edition began, "Dear Readers and Riders: Well it finally happened! So many letters I didn't know what to do. I felt exactly like the old woman in the shoe. Here were children's letters full of questions so exciting that each one required a special answer." At the bottom of the page is a photograph in profile of Marguerite reading a letter with a mound of fan mail covering her desk. At its highest point, the stack of letters reached about eighteen inches high.

That inaugural newsletter had two articles: "Brighty Becomes a Movie Star," and "The Story Behind the Lipizzan Story," along with responses to six fan letters covering questions such as how long it took her to write a book, and whether or not the book *Sea Star* was true (it is "based almost wholly on fact").

My favorite letter read, "Dear Miss Henry, I have a question to ask you if you don't mind. Do you think it is right to kiss a horse on the nose which you love dearly?"

Her response: "If he doesn't object, why not?"

Fan mail continued to roll in. In the ninth edition of the newsletter, Marguerite announced that Peg Guild, a letter writer from Wheaton, Illinois, gave her a wonderful suggestion: "Why don't you take the questions children and adults have asked you and make a question-and-answer book." In 1969 Rand McNally released *Dear Readers and Riders*, with a subsequent edition titled *Dear Marguerite Henry*.

Newsletter No. 9 explained her new book was dedicated "to every one of you who have ever written a letter to me. Even if your specific question is not included, you have contributed to the book because you took the time to sit down and write out your thoughts and feelings about reading and writing, and horses and riding, and foxes and burros, all manner of things."

With the letters, children often sent Marguerite pictures. I opened one file folder and, like dealing out a massive deck of cards, arranged all its photographs on the table. A sea of one hundred eighty-one wallet-sized school pictures smirked, smiled or stared seriously back at me, a mosaic of horse lovers spanning decades. There were a few black and white photos of girls wearing cat eye glasses and some in John Lennon-style wire rims. Many of the snapshots were aged and yellowed color photos from the 1960s. The 1970s were represented by long butterfly collars and feathered hair. From Pensacola, Florida and Seattle, Washington to Linden, New Jersey and St. Paul, Minnesota, each photo symbolized admiration and fandom.

The pictures spread out before me represented just one folder: number two of ten. If that one photo container was representative of the other nine, Marguerite had saved around eighteen hundred school photos from children.

I turned many of the photos over to read what was written on the back. One little girl's school picture read,

"To Mrs. Henry,

I sure look bad, right?

Thanks so much for caring enough to write me back.

P.S. Drop the 'Miss' please!

Love ya! Patty Kelly"

A school photograph from a Houston fan read, "To My Pen Pal Marguerite Henry, From Rhoda Lanier. Thanks for helping me earn my Pen Pal Badge in Girl Scouts." I'm not sure if I was more delighted at the bold request of a girl engaging a famous author to be her pen pal or the fact that Marguerite was game to respond.

Another school picture read, "I feel I've known you a long time! Your friend Sandy." In mature handwriting, in black marker, the name "Gerber" was squeezed vertically on the back of the photo. Marguerite's fan mattered enough to her to include her last name, thus differentiating her from the other countless school photos. This was a pattern: if the child had only written their first name, Marguerite added the child's last name. I pictured her checking the letter's signature or perhaps return address to piece together the full name. I thought about how that small detail of keeping names straight showed thoughtfulness and caring.

In addition to the school photos, I found many snapshots of children with horses, frequently named Misty or Stormy. One horse photo gave me warm fuzzies: it showed a thick palomino with ears at half-mast and a smiling pigtailed cowgirl in tan and gold wearing jack-o'-lantern orange bows around her hair and neck. She beams from under her straw hat. The message on the back of the photo read, "Patches and I at horse show (we didn't place)." In pencil Marguerite wrote the name of the girl, Vickie Vandervoort, along with, "You placed in my heart." The word heart is underlined.

On occasion, entire classes would write to Marguerite. A 1979 letter from a teacher in Massachusetts read, "When you saw this postmark, I'm certain you thought, 'This is a familiar town!' Obviously, my students read and enjoyed *Misty*, which prompted the 'flood' of letters you received recently. As their teacher, I wanted to write and say thank you for your replies. The children realize how lucky they are to have received personal replies from you, and have eagerly shared those replies with all of us. Few people care to take the time these days, particularly when children are concerned. But we truly appreciate your thoughtfulness and we say thank you, from all of us."

Lauren Hoeffer, a Breyer model horse enthusiast from Arizona, wrote Marguerite a letter in 1995 asking if she had a favorite book of those she had written. Lauren received an envelope from California with the faces of the six horses from Marguerite's letterhead. Marguerite, then ninety-two, replied, "I don't have a favorite book. I'm like a mother with many children. I love each book-child for a different and very special reason."

Marguerite not only loved each book-child, but also the children who wrote her or befriended her in real life. The closing paragraph of the last edition of her fan newsletter said of the forthcoming *Dear Readers and Riders*, "Wherever you read the book—in your home or at your library—I hope you will know at once that it was written for you; it is my way of saying, I love you."

The illustrator Bonnie Shields, who collaborated with Marguerite on *Brown Sunshine of Sawdust Valley*, and was kind enough to draw two originals for this book (see the chapter headings and page 66) loved Marguerite too. Bonnie, known as the Tennessee Mule Artist even though she's lived in Idaho for decades, is in her early eighties. During their first introduction, Bonnie was star struck as she had read most of Marguerite's horse books growing up.

"I met Marguerite Henry in the parking lot of a motel in Columbia, Tennessee. And I mean, we looked at each other and it was like we knew each other. We just knew each other."

Bonnie continued, "You would be amazed. Even at her age in her nineties, she got letters and letters and letters from little children. And they would all put a little drawing in it and she had them posted up in her office. She was always changing them because she was getting them forever. But they were always there, and she always got a lot of delight out of them. She was the real thing, honey. She was the real thing."

In the late 1960s, a boy from Oregon wrote Marguerite divulging that his father had gotten rid of his best friend, his horse, without telling him.

Marguerite wanted to help the heartbroken boy in the only way she felt she could. We learn in her short film *Story of a Book* that she decided she would write a book just for him. She based the main character, a brave Pony Express rider named Peter Lundy, on that hurting boy. She elevated her fan to hero status in *San Domingo: Medicine Hat Stallion*.

Perhaps that was Marguerite's secret of success as an author: a heart filled with love.

13

INFLUENCE BEFORE INFLUENCERS WERE A THING

After illustrator Wesley Dennis' death in 1966, Marguerite stopped writing for a year. When the story of Velma Johnston, a Nevada secretary who fought for protection of wild Mustangs, enticed the author to return to writing, Marguerite needed an illustrator. She wooed Robert Lougheed, a fine art painter, into illustrating her next two titles. Lougheed, whose oil paintings graced the pages of *National Geographic* and today can be found in the National Cowboy and Western Heritage Museum and art galleries, collaborated with Marguerite on *Mustang: Wild Spirit of the West* and *San Domingo: Medicine Hat Stallion*.

While researching the Marguerite Henry archival documents from the quiet of the University of Minnesota's Elmer Anderson Library, I felt an autumn breeze blow me to a Wyoming Spanish Mustang ranch. I read Marguerite's October 20, 1967, letter to Mary Alice Jones.

"One wild, windy morning, Robert Lougheed, Bob Brislawn and I climbed to a buffalo stand on the pinnacle of the world and watched herds of horses come bursting up from the valleys, come galloping up and up across the swells of the hills closer and closer until the earth quaked beneath our feet. He knows each by name, knows their sires and dams, often their grandsires and great grandsires."

Marguerite, Robert Lougheed, and Cordy, Robert's wife, had convened at Cayuse Ranch in Wyoming, home of cowboy and wild horse advocate Bob Brislawn. Marguerite described him as "the gentle little crickety old man in a high-crowned cowboy hat that all but swallows him."

In thirty seasons as a surveyor, crossing the rugged landscape of the American West, Brislawn learned the ways of wild horses, and the progeny of the Conquistador steeds stole his heart. Bob traveled to Canada, Mexico, Montana and beyond to locate and purchase Spanish Mustangs in order to preserve them. He did not want the bloodlines of the sturdy, affectionate horses to become diluted or die out. He brought them home to Cayuse Ranch in Oshoto, Wyoming and created the Spanish Mustang Registry in 1957. Brislawn also published *Cimarron*, a newsletter about wild horses, and Marguerite was a subscriber.

After the ranch trip letter, I began reading correspondence between Marguerite and Brislawn, who I learned during his days as a surveyor in the 1920s met and befriended a man who was tracking buffalo. The man turned out to be a relative of the infamous villain Jesse James.

As interesting as the cowboy's old-timey anecdotes were, a revelation as exciting as a herd of Mustangs galloping toward me materialized.

Marguerite and Robert Lougheed bought two Spanish Mustang fillies from Brislawn and donated them to the National Cowboy Hall of Fame in Oklahoma City.

In a November 3, 1967 letter, to Sanford Cobb of Rand McNally, Marguerite wrote that while she and Robert Lougheed were in Oklahoma City accepting a Western Heritage Award for *Mustang,* Dean Krakel, managing director of the museum, shared his vision of establishing a living museum. He wanted a place where children could see elk, buffalo and a true Mustang. Marguerite and Lougheed had not given the living museum comment another thought until the day at Cayuse Ranch when, "we stood atop that buffalo stand and saw Mr. Brislawn's pure specimens. Then we completely lost our hearts and minds. It came to us with a bang that we two had been 'chosen' to donate the mustangs to the children's new museum. Mr. Brislawn seemed joyous to be part of the doings. He gave us a ridiculously low price of $100 each and $50 for shipping. Bob [Robert Lougheed] and I are sure that families who are horse-show-minded would pay $1,000 apiece for them. That same night with Cordy cheering us on, we wrote out our checks."

I sat up straighter in the library chair and reread the passage.

In another letter dated October 4, 1967 to Mr. Mustang, Marguerite wrote, "We are so happy that the name BRISLAWN and CAYUSE RANCH will now appear in the National Cowboy Hall of Fame, for if anyone is preserving a symbol of the past for all the children of the earth it is you."

How is it I had never heard or read anything about this before? There is no mention of it in Marguerite's newsletters, which were published concurrently with the horse donation. *Dear Marguerite Henry* said nothing about it either. In later research I came across a single mention of the Mustang in a 1968 interview now on YouTube. The interviewer asked Marguerite if she currently had a horse and she said no, but explained how she and Robert had purchased Mustangs for the museum. She went on to say she and Sidney had been offered two Lipizzaners, and, "I'm at that stage where I'm trying to convince my husband we need two Lipizzanners more than anything in the world."

I lost myself in more letters. In one, Marguerite reported to Brislawn that she received an update from Dean Krakel, the museum director. "The fillies are doing very well ... they make quite a sight next to old Abilene. They have been spooky but seem to be settling down. By next summer we want to put them in our corral for the public to get to know."

Not to be confused with the city in Texas, Abilene was a Texas Longhorn steer with a horn spread of eight feet donated to the museum by an Oklahoma businessman. The steer, a public relations ambassador, is commemorated today with a grave marker in a livestock graveyard on the grounds of the National Cowboy and Western Heritage Museum.

In another letter, Marguerite told Brislawn that if he made a trip to Oklahoma City later that spring he would meet Mac "who is caring for 'our' mustangs ... he impressed me as being a great horseman, with a real love and understanding of their needs and potentialities." Marguerite's donated Spanish Mustang was a buckskin she named Yellow Wings and the Lougheeds' was Redwing.

For a woman who was so great at promoting horses and her books, why was she seemingly quiet on the Spanish Mustang donation? The answer dawned on me: the Marguerite I had gotten to know was simultaneously influential and humble.

I remembered finding her cursive in the margin on a draft of an autobiography she had written for an author anthology declaring, "I have never read anything so bumptious and presumptuous." I had to look up the meaning of "bumptious" and learned it means "self-assertive or proud to an irritating degree." I had also read a column she wrote for the education journal *California English*. Above the article titled "Rewriting: I Do It My Way," the familiar handwriting scrawled, "I've never read anything more smugly pompous. Keep it only entre nous." The word "keep" was crossed out with the word "destroy" inserted in its place.

This on-the-down-low gift was right in line with her character. Of course she would purchase a horse and give it away to a museum where children and adults would see, smell, and perhaps even touch living history.

***

"Please pretend that I'm about eight years old and tell me what happens when a stallion is about to be shown at the stockyards, just how they line up and who's in it. Would you tell me a little bit?" This was one of many questions Marguerite asked during a 1951 phone interview with Andy Haxton, the manager and driver of the famous Budweiser Clydesdale hitch. Marguerite had typed a transcript of her interview during her research on Clydesdales for *Album of Horses*.

Mr. Haxton responded in short, to-the-point answers. Marguerite peppered him with more questions, perhaps hoping to tease out the lively details she was known for. By the end of the interview, thanks to Marguerite's determined curiosity, Haxton opened up, describing the art of showing Clydesdale stallions in hand, explaining every aspect from the initial line-up to trotting, and concluding with the judge's soundness exams.

As I read the complete transcript, I realized the exchange between interviewer and interviewee highlights one of Marguerite's special attributes: no matter her age—she was forty-nine at the time—she viewed the world through the eyes of a child. Her audience was rooted in the forefront of her mind as she researched, which inspired her to collect details that would capture their interest.

In 1960, Marguerite wrote a letter to Roland Lindemann, owner of the Catskill Game Farm, in her attempt to find the locations of all the Przewalski's horses in the U.S. for her 1962 release, *All About Horses*. Marguerite stated, "I am including a chapter on the one and only true wild horse. It seems to me that many of the boys and girls who read the book might want to know where they could actually see a wild horse, and I am planning to mention the places." She said she knew of the two Przewalski's at the Brookfield Zoo in Chicago and one at the National Zoo in Washington D.C. She was curious if he had any in New York.

In *All About Horses*, one paragraph tucked into the one hundred twenty-four-page treasury of horse history from Eohippus to warmbloods tells readers where to find the "dull, dark yellow, lighter on the sides than on the back, and almost cream colored on the belly" Przewalski's horses. Besides Lindemann's farm, the Brookfield Zoo, and the National Zoo, the wild and wooly horses could be found in Central Park: at the New York Zoological Gardens. I wonder how many young horse lovers close to New York and Chicago begged their parents to take them to see the wild Przewalski's thanks to Marguerite's recommendation.

***

Marguerite was serious and research-oriented, but equally warm, fun and hospitable. Long before a cardigan-wearing Fred Rogers took to the airwaves in *Mr. Roger's Neighborhood* valuing the dignity of children, teaching them they were special and loved, Marguerite broadcast an identical message through her books, letters, and in person. She lived out a line from Mr. Rogers' song, "Won't you be my neighbor," by welcoming children to her neighborhood and home.

Ann Keckonen of Sheboygan, Wisconsin, a distant relative of Sidney Henry I found via Ancestry.com, met her famous relative a few times in person. Ann was a child the first time she met Marguerite and got to ride Misty. Ann and Marguerite connected again in 1978 when Ann's daughter wanted to meet the famous writer to whom she was related. "She was a lovely, friendly lady, and she considered all the children who visited her and Misty to be her children." Marguerite's warmth endeared her to fans. If she were alive today and active on social media, my guess is she would have hundreds of thousands—perhaps millions—of ardent followers.

Marguerite was decades ahead of the times in what is now commonplace on social media: animal influencers. Today, there are popular social media accounts of animals with distinct personalities and roles. For example, in France, Peyo, a gallant chestnut gelding, on Instagram as @docteur_peyo, makes hospital visits to lift the spirits of patients. Another equine influencer, Endo, a blind Appaloosa featured by his person Morgan at @endotheblind.morgan, navigates wooded trails and teaches tiny equestrians how to ride, proving blind horses still have much to give. And who could forget Grumpy Cat, the feline who frowned her way to Internet fame in the early 2010s while putting smiles on our faces?

Marguerite and Misty would fit right in today's social media landscape as the author and pony continually connected with their audience. They visited schools, libraries and department stores in order to sign books, stage skits, and meet fans.

It's not clear if Misty's appearances were the brainchild of Marguerite or publisher Rand McNally, but I discovered a possible clue in Chicago's Newberry Library: two photos of exotic animal publicity appearances. The first is a November 1944 photograph of an elephant in the middle of Marshall Fields with a tasseled cape draped across its back emblazoned with Eddie the Elegant Elephant. The three thousand-pound creature was actually Judy, a female who held a hand stamp in her trunk and "signed" copies of the picture book *The Elegant Elephant*. I thought it was hilarious when I read that Judy was reluctant to leave the store and ate the Indian corn on store displays before exiting.

Another Rand McNally photo shows a pretty young woman with backcombed hair holding on her hip a chimpanzee wearing oxfords, dressed in slacks and a shirt with the name "Zip" spelled out in all caps. The ape was the star of the 1953 book *Zippy the Chimp*. Misty's appearances began after Eddie/Judy the elephant and ran concurrently with Zippy, who, incidentally, roller skated, smoked a cigarette and rode a bicycle on the *Ed Sullivan Show*. With those photos providing context, Misty meet ups seem right in line with Rand McNally marketing of that era. Although Misty never appeared on Ed Sullivan, she went on the road to promote the film inspired by her life. In true Hollywood starlet fashion, she left hoof imprints on the sidewalk in front of the

Chincoteague Island movie theater. You can see them in the concrete today.

Marguerite wielded influence to engage with and elevate others, as well as to promote causes she was passionate about. Her winsome ways appealed to children and adults, and as a result, a strong community rose around her. In a 1951 radio interview promoting *Album of Horses*, Marguerite said, "Misty has a birthday party every July 20th. I never send any invitations but everybody is invited ... Children can see her and she shakes hands, and then always she has to have a little handout of oats."

On air, she invited Wesley Dennis, who was joining her in the studio, to come to the birthday party. He declined, stating, "That's the middle of summer. I'm always trying to catch a fish at that time."

"Well, you might catch a birthday cake with carrot tops for candles," Marguerite teased.

Local newspapers would run articles about the pony's upcoming birthday, and fans sent a "shower of greeting cards" addressed simply to Misty at Mole Meadow. Marguerite posted the pony birthday cards on the wall of Misty's stable declaring, "She seemed to enjoy looking them over."

Publisher's Weekly reported on Misty's seventh birthday party. "This year there were almost 400 guests, and they brought Misty tributes which included a set of gold-plated horse shoe nails, 84 bunches of carrots and quantities of sugar lumps, apples and cookies."

Each child received a piece of chocolate cake baked in a horseshoe mold, and Misty received a birthday cake made of oats, sugar, molasses, chopped walnuts and carrots turned upside down as candles. The recipe for Misty's Oat Cake is found on page 50 of *A Pictorial Life Story of Misty*. One of these days I will make it for my horse. It sounds delicious.

Much to my delight, the Kerlan Collection at the University of Minnesota had a digitized version of a 16-millimeter black-and-white home movie from a pony birthday party!

I've now lost track of how many times I've watched the one-minute undated pony party film. It begins with a sweeping panorama of Mole Meadow. Behind the rows of party guests, a sea of elementary age children are seated on grass, a long stream of cars lining the distant road. The Henrys' front lawn had a low depression that made for a natural amphitheater; the top of the slope was a prime location for fans to witness the antics of Misty and friends on "center stage," where Misty held court.

The film shows the pony, front hooves planted on the top of her stool, with young boys at each shoulder. In the next scene, one boy sits atop Misty's white patch. The second boy, wearing a blonde wig and a skirt over his jeans portraying Maureen Beebe, leads a floral-garland-wearing Misty around. I showed the footage to Ed Richardson, the man who accompanied Marguerite on trail rides when he was a boy. He was the one in the wig as Maureen!

After the Misty pageant, Jiggs and a man with fluffy fake white eyebrows playing the role of Uncle Jim, act out the reunification scene in *Brighty*. If you've never read *Brighty*, or it's been a while, Brighty the burro narrowly escapes drowning in the Colorado River. Following his near-death experience, the battered burro journeys to his friend Uncle Jim, who nurses him back to health. In the pony party film, the man playing Uncle Jim throws a blanket over the burro and pretends to pour cough syrup down his throat. I later read when Jiggs played Brighty's role, his legs were bloodied with ketchup to show the fierceness of his fight. "He couldn't help licking the catsup, which always brought down the house."

In the movie, just before Marguerite leads the birthday honoree back to her stall, she presents Misty the carrot-candled cake. The movie doesn't show Misty eating the cake, but I would have loved to have seen that.

As much as she delighted in pony parties and Misty meetups, Marguerite was not just about having fun. Beyond celebrations and special events, Marguerite used her influence to both educate and mobilize children to become civically active members of society. After the success of her 1966 book *Mustang, Wild Spirit of the West*, which she wrote with the help of Bob Brislawn, featuring Wild Horse Annie, Marguerite ignited a children's letter-writing campaign on behalf of Mustangs. She recognized the vital role America's wild horses played in shaping our nation's history, and her role in telling their story for future generations. Wild Horse Annie wrote a letter to Brislawn stating, "Mrs. Henry's book *Mustang, Wild Spirit of the West* has become a powerful tool in disseminating the news about the plight of the wild ones."

In Marguerite's Spring 1967 newsletter, she shared that men were caught chasing wild horses by plane, breaking Public Law 86-234, the Wild Horse Annie Act of 1959. The author urged readers, "You can help. Everybody can. Write to the Bureau of Land Management in Washington, D. C., reminding its members that there is a Federal Bill that forbids the horrible roundup of wild horses by plane, and that you, the boys and girls of our nation, ask that the law-enforcers uphold it." And write they did.

A year later, the fall 1968 newsletter began, "Dear determined letter writers, I am glad, proud, and grateful to all of you for the new explosion of letters you sent to the Bureau of Land Management about the wild horses up in the Pryor Mountains ... the way you peppered the Bureau with our protests and pleas has brought a big victory."

Next she inserted a copy of a telegram from the BLM's Office of Information into the letter, stating that the Secretary of the Interior, Stewart L. Udall, and the BLM had set aside a 31,000-acre wildlife range in the Pryor Mountains along the Montana-Wyoming border to protect wild horses. (Today the range is 39,000 acres.) The most striking line in the BLM's telegram was its conclusion: "We all recognize these horses are national asset, and this herd is suitable to management of the wild horse so important to western history." The law stands to this day.

Marguerite's efforts encouraging children to write and advocate for wild horses didn't stop with the range in the Pryor Mountains. In her next newsletter she asked readers to write letters to the new Secretary of the Interior, Walter J. Hickel, urging him to set aside a refuge for the Mustangs near the Colorado-Utah border in the Book Cliffs mountains.

Today pintos and palominos, blue and red roans, bays, grays, sorrels, blacks, and a few Appaloosas frolic in the Little Book Cliffs Wild Horse Area, a 36,000-acre range just outside Grand Junction, Colorado. The countless young letter writers' desires became a reality.

14

CHINCOTEAGUE PONY SUPERFANS

"It all started with Marguerite," said Chincoteague Pony owner Allison Dotzel when I asked her to share how she came to own her pony. When Allison, a veterinarian from Pennsylvania, was starting out in her career, she shared with a close friend, "I think I might want to get one of those ponies someday."

Her friend asked her, "Why wait? Why not get one now?"

That set Allison to thinking. Her Quarter Horse mare was in her mid twenties, and it made sense to get a young horse as it would take time to bring it along. The idea grew on her. Allison, who has read *Misty of Chincoteague* at least twenty times, got to live out the story, taking part in the real live auction portrayed in the book. Allison was the highest bidder on a flashy chestnut pinto colt at the 2015 Pony Penning Week auction. The pony, Finn, is now her horse show partner and dream come true.

Finn, a taller representative of Chincoteague ponies, stands 14.1 hands high and is twenty-five percent Arab from when Arabians were released into the herd in the 1990s.

"You'd be surprised at how fancy some of them are. They did neat things with bloodlines by adding Mustangs and Arabians into the herd, creating interesting outcrosses which has made them a really versatile pony. I showed my guy Finn at the Pinto World Show. He was not out of place with other horses. He does well in halter against Quarter Horses," Allison said.

The strategic introduction of new bloodlines into the herd was just one of the many fun facts I learned about the ponies from Allison.

"A lot of people have Misty in the back of their minds when they figure out the pony swim is still going on. It's not overly commercialized, and Chincoteague still has a small-town feel. The way they do the auction is still the same. Cowboys bring foals out and you raise your hand to bid."

As Allison spoke, I typed notes as fast as I could, ingesting every morsel of Chincoteague Pony data. At the time of our conversation, there were nineteen stallions on the island, but not all of them had bands, as some of them were still too young. Clusters of young stallions kicked out of the band they were born into hang out together with other young stallions in bachelor bands until they are mature enough to woo mares and begin their own bands. Thirty ponies live in the southern area of Assateague, and the rest of them stick to the more remote, northern area. In order to see ponies of the northern territory you must hike up a seven-and-a-half mile long service road.

The ease with which Allison spoke of the herd of 150 free-roaming ponies, and citing names of Misty descendants was impressive. The facility of her pony sharing was akin to someone with a large family of cousins, aunts and uncles discussing family goings on. It also reminded me of speaking to an NBA fan, or any sports lover, who can name all-stars, and spout off team win-loss stats, player trades, positions played, and colleges attended.

My mind was blown.

Allison was a fount of knowledge. I discovered the wild ponies are also rounded up on Assateague every spring and fall in order to receive veterinary care. Pony fans converge on the island to see the bands for that too, but it's much less crowded than Pony Penning Week in July. I knew the Chincoteague Volunteer Fire Company owned the island herd, but I discovered their level of involvement is more hands-on than I would have guessed based on watching the July pony swim on a news segment or past Pony Penning clips on YouTube.

For example, it's a little-known fact that not all ponies make the summer swim: mares too pregnant, foals too young or horses too old are exempt, and are trailered to the Chincoteague carnival grounds, the site of the foal auction. Although Allison said the newborn foals can swim, eyewitnesses frequently see them sloshing in the water and gliding behind their dams. If an island pony is struggling to keep on weight, the fire department will trailer it the short distance from Assateague over to Chincoteague and feed it. If they see one limping, they'll bring it over to Chincoteague for veterinary care.

Every year a committee composed of Chincoteague Volunteer Fire Company Members meets to determine which foals will be auctioned off to individual homes and which foals will be auctioned but returned to the island after they are sold. The foals who are purchased for naming rights and then returned to the island are referred to as "buybacks."

Usually, the committee chooses fillies as buybacks. The foals' color and bloodlines influence the decision. The committee also determines a cut-off date for those old enough to go home by the time of the auction or decides if they need to be picked up during the fall roundup in October. Every colt or filly born by July is sold, but the younger ones will be allowed more time to grow up alongside their dams. Even though it may seem like any random person can bid on and potentially win a pony, winning bidders are subject to the review of the Chincoteague Volunteer Fire Company.

In 2018, a number of ponies on the island were affected by equine pythiosis, a condition sometimes called "swamp cancer." Pythiosis is not actually cancer, but a rare disease contracted by standing in or near stagnant freshwater such as a swamp or lake. A red, oozy lesion will develop that, if not treated, can be fatal. In 2021, ponies were sent to Oklahoma for treatment from a veterinarian pioneering a vaccine for the condition. Chincoteague ponies who were vaccinated but still contracted pythiosis helped to improve the treatments and efficacy of the vaccine.

People follow the herd and want to support the ponies, and it's also a tax write-off, as the money goes toward the Chincoteague Volunteer Fire Company, a nonprofit organization. Allison said often friends get together and pool money to purchase a buyback pony and gain naming rights. "People are excited about their part in the history of the pony." Although they don't keep the pony, buyback purchasers are photographed with the foals.

What makes the ponies so appealing, beyond the sentimentality of *Misty of Chincoteague,* is their versatility. Allison said, "I've seen them cut cows, event, drive, and be used for 4-H, trail and companion. They do just about everything."

During our forty-minute phone conversation, Allison's Chincoteague Pony stories were so compelling, I moved "Go to Pony Penning Week" to the top of my "Marguerite and Misty Research To-Do" list. I needed to see firsthand the ponies by the sea, and experience the wonder of the event Marguerite called the Wild West show of the East—the pageant that brought the *Misty* books to life.

***

I found Allison through Tara, a fellow horse blogger who is a foxhunter and dog rescuer from Texas. Tara readily admits she uses whether a person has read Marguerite Henry books as a litmus test of just how horsey they are. In 2020, Tara's horse girl dream was realized when she and her best friend bid on a solid chestnut colt with a dash of a star on his forehead. They won the bid and a Chincoteague Pony they named Ginuwine Lefty II, nicknamed "Gene," trotted into their lives.

When I first reached out to Tara via Instagram to ask if she would be willing to talk to me about her Chincoteague Pony and help me connect with other Chincoteague Pony owners, her reply? "Yes. It's a cult."

Tara grew up on a ranch in Montana, and even though she was surrounded by horses—her parents bred Quarter Horses—she had always wanted a foal of her very own. Tara's longing was just like that of Paul and Maureen Beebe, the protagonists in *Misty*. Although the brother and sister lived on a pony farm with their grandparents, they longed to have a horse of their own.

The Pony Penning auction the year Tara and friend bid on Gene was held online because of the pandemic. No excited families, nor lifelong Misty fans were in attendance. Typically, the event takes place on the island to much fanfare. Tens of thousands of pony superfans line the shore as the Saltwater Cowboys drive the Virginia herd from Assateague to Chincoteague for the roundup and sale.

Tara informed me that all of the Chincoteague Ponies on the island have names, and a team of photographers hike the island every day during foaling season to get precise records of foals' births. Bloodlines of the ponies are kept by the International Chincoteague Pony Association and Registry on an open community database, the Chincoteague Pony Pedigree Database. It sounded like the community of Chincoteague owners and fans is tight knit—as though everyone knew everyone.

Sometime after the revelation that all the wild Chincoteague Ponies have names, I discovered a Chincoteague Pony Names app. The app is useful for in-person viewing of the herd on Assateague, or if you can't make it to that part of the world but want to follow the ponies.

A search wizard lets you click on options like gender, color, brand, face, leg and pinto markings. Once you've made your selections such as female, bay, no face marking, for example, a list of names will appear. You can then scroll through pictures and videos of horses to help identify a particular pony. When the desired pony is located, by tapping on "Family," a family tree will appear. Horses related to Misty have a special notation on their pedigree. The Android version's revenue is donated to the Chincoteague Pony Rescue.

One night at a burger joint, I showed a fellow equestrian the app; she immediately bought it. We middle-aged horse lovers might not play Candy Crush, but now we can follow our own Chincoteague Pony crushes conveniently from our phones.

Just as Marguerite and Misty played a role in putting Chincoteague on the map in the late 1940s, social media platforms continue to keep the ponies on the forefront of horse lovers' minds making them desirable. In 2021, a buyback pony sold for $25,000 and it's not unusual for those selected to be released on the island to live in freedom to garner prices in that range. The highest-selling foal at the time of this writing was a 2022 pony at $32,000.

***

Darcy Cole reminds me a little bit of the Jane Goodall of the Chincoteague Ponies. Camera in hand, she has spent the better part of the last decade hiking Assateague, recording meticulous notes on the herds and their doings. With no formal background in biology but a heart-filled with love for animals, when the amateur photographer discovered that each island pony had a name, it set her interest in them ablaze. I learned about Darcy through Tara, and began following her very active Facebook page DSC Photography.

"I had a horse named Misty and when I came here, I didn't get hooked on the ponies until I found out they had names. Once I found out, that flicker of a flame turned into an inferno—a thirst for knowledge that can't be quenched. I started learning about which mares were with which stallions and I have breeding sighting documents. I have so much data and track so much it could be research for a dissertation with all kinds of charts and graphs. Most foals are born in May, then April and then June. The last foal will be born in November. It's a bell curve." Darcy has no interest in going back to school in pursuit of a doctoral degree. She just loves the ponies.

"I got pony fever in 2013, but started documenting in 2015. I have pictures of all the stallions and mares. At first it was so overwhelming, but

I now know them like family with their unique personalities. There is so much joy just sitting there and watching the foals play. Last year we had eighty-three born. This year I think there will be seventy to seventy-five."

Three hundred days out of the year, Darcy hikes Assateague Island to observe and perhaps commune with the ponies. A few days prior to our phone conversation, she had spent six hours waiting for the perfect shot of a foal.

Darcy photographs them with a 400mm lens, allowing her to keep a respectful distance from the wild ponies. She began a Facebook Page dedicated to posting pony pictures. Today she is an admin for her page and private Facebook Groups.

Her work capturing images and detailed notes of the ponies is a kind of personal mission. "I'm a cancer survivor and this is how I want to spend the rest of my life. It's a passion and a calling. I was ready to give up and then people started telling us how we helped get them through COVID. They could come to our page, and it was the best thing on Facebook." She likens her 8 a.m., noon, and 4 p.m. daily posts of cute foals from the island to television programming and has not missed a day in the last two years.

Darcy's husband hikes the island with her on his days off work. He has been snapping photos for thirty years while Darcy began photography in 2015. As the couple started sharing their pony photos on Facebook, people began asking to purchase them. Today, they have a website where the photos can be purchased for framing, digital use, or made into keepsakes such as refrigerator magnets, puzzles or coffee mugs.

In addition to being passionate about documenting the herd, she has jumped headlong into buyback pony ownership, as a result of being smitten by the foals. Since 2015 she has purchased thirty-eight of them.

"I'm collecting every color. We fall in love with the foals. You want to be a part of watching them grow up and be a part of their naming." Her first purchase was in 2015 when she was part of a group of four hundred people who pooled funds to pay $25,000 for Blue Moon (full name CLG Surfer's Blue Moon) a black filly sporting a wide blaze and sapphire eyes.

Darcy believes the draw of buyback ownership is that it allows people the joy of watching a foal grow up, and, of course, participate in choosing a name. Out of the various groups she has taken part in for buyback ponies, Darcy's names were chosen twice: Rider on the Storm and Tomorrow's Tidewater Twist. Each year she typically helps one or two families who can't finance a buyback on their own. Usually the buyback is in memory of somebody, and they have an interesting story or name.

Darcy shared anecdotes with me that further solidified Allison's point that the Chincoteague Volunteer Fire Company takes their role as herd stewards seriously. "They come like 911 [does] for a person. It's unbelievable. I heard about this story from a lady who was at church when this happened. All of a sudden, the Saltwater Cowboys got up out of church to rescue a colt that was stuck in mud."

With hip boots over their Sunday clothes, the volunteer firefighters pulled the imperiled colt out of the mire. Once the foal was freed, they rubbed his legs to stimulate circulation, and waited around to observe him. They wanted to ensure his digestive and urinary systems functioned after the distress. The colt was fine.

Another time a stallion got banged up—they're not sure what happened, maybe a tree branch fell on him—and they stitched up his ear. That was the stud Ajax. In 2022 the bay pinto with white withers, tied with Don Leonard Stud II for siring the most foals, nine apiece. Apparently Ajax was none the worse for wear.

Darcy is one example in a long line of passionate pony documentarians. From the early 2000s until her death in 2017, Kelly Lidard followed the herd and wrote three books that were field guides to the ponies. The late pony historian left behind tens of thousands of photos and at least thirty-two personal photo albums based on her hikes and observations on Assateague. Before Kelly, Deb Noll photographed the ponies starting in 1978. Around 2010, Kathleen and Dick Cahall from Ohio started following the ponies, donating two buyback ponies: Skylark and Lorna Dune. Kathleen is considered the go-to person for information on conformation and physical traits. In 2022 she hiked three and a half miles up and three and a half miles back for the northern herd roundup on Assateague—in a hurricane.

***

While searching through archival material at the University of Minnesota, I happened upon an undated scrap of paper with Marguerite's handwriting that read, "The dynasty of Misty will continue as long as there are children who remember the golden pony with the map of the U.S. on her withers." Henry's words rang true, and as I connected with equine devotees whose hearts beat in rhythm with the ponies who ride the waves, the cult comment Tara joked about made sense. This is one "cult" whose members I hope are never deprogrammed. Delight and belonging is what the ponies offer people. Each glimpse of ponies playing in the sea or lounging on the sand, and every rowdy foal is something to behold, whether seen in real life or via photos and videos online or an app. Their very existence evokes joy, and if you love them, you are automatically part of a larger community.

I checked my calendar to see how many weeks there were before Pony Penning, and joined the Chincoteague's Riptide Facebook group, a community of fans who adore the liver chestnut stud with blond locks that drape past his shoulder and halfway down his face. I realized this hardcore Thoroughbred fan was falling for the ponies too. I booked a flight to the East Coast to follow on the trail of Marguerite and the herd that she made famous.

15

PONY PENNING PRELUDE

As I drove onto the causeway, I tilted my sunglasses down to see if the polarization was intensifying the brilliant marsh colors. Swaths of shimmering water intermixed with lanky blades of almost chartreuse grass. White egrets on stilt legs strode along areas of low tide murk. Dozens of billboards for local businesses greeted me on the left-hand side of the road to this mythical place, Chincoteague Island. The earliest residents who named this place the "beautiful land across the water" described it perfectly.

For many Misty fans, going to Chincoteague is a life goal. It was something I had thought about once in a while for the past several years. When I read the books as a child, it didn't occur to me I could actually visit Virginia, not because it was mythical, just impractical. Tweens don't travel without family, and mine wasn't big on vacations, unless you count the

Illinois State Fair in Springfield. But as an adult, I knew I couldn't write authentically about my muse and her famous pony without a pilgrimage to the destination where their timeless story began.

In *Dear Marguerite Henry*, the author described Chincoteague Island's annual Pony Penning.

"All year long wild pinto ponies roam free on Assateague Island. Then along comes Pony Penning Day, and a bunch of men who were fisherfolk yesterday turn cowboy today. Loading their own horses on a scow, they cross over from Chincoteague to Assateague and put on the biggest Wild West show in the East! Through marsh and bog and briar they ride hard and fast, spooking the wild ones out of hiding, driving them to Toms Cove. It's like a tidal wave seeping all the ponies to one spot where they can blow and catch their breath ... the water churns with ponies—stallions bugling to their mares, mare neighing to the colts." After the pony swim, which she watched from a boat, the cowboys drove the slick ponies right down Main Street to the Carnival Grounds.

Pony Penning Week is like Christmas, New Year's, and the Fourth of July all rolled into one. It's an annual week-long celebration when the Virginia herd of wild ponies on Assateague are rounded up and swim across the channel to neighboring Chincoteague. Thousands of spectators from near and far gather to view the wild ponies. I needed to see it for myself.

At first I wasn't keen on visiting Chincoteague during Pony Penning week because of the crowds. I heard the ponies were also rounded up in spring and fall in order to have their overall health assessed and note if any other foals were born. I thought spring or fall would be the best fit for me. After leaving California, I had hit my life's quota for sitting in traffic. There was a time I traveled four Southern California freeways and seventy-five miles one way to see Knight. People thought I was nuts for my three-hour round-trip barn commute. They didn't understand how Knight had space to stretch his legs, was turned out in a field sixteen hours a day, and was the healthiest he'd been in my years owning him. If my horse was happy, I flexed to his lifestyle, as much as I despised the traffic congestion.

I had heard island traffic was crazy, so I decided that instead of Pony Penning week, I would opt for the calmer fall roundup in October. I would still get to see the ponies, and hopefully the hordes would stay home. But a friend's wedding on the West Coast the same weekend as the fall roundup necessitated a travel plan pivot. July it was.

In 2022, with less than three weeks until the blessed event when Chincoteague's population of about three thousand balloons by thousands, I remarkably found not just an available hotel room, but a kayak to rent for the Pony Swim from Assateague to Chincoteague. To top it off, I reserved a spot on a boat ride for the Friday swim back to freedom!

I turned right onto Main Street, driving slowly to take it all in. On the right, a tall painted sign for Chincotiki Bar and Grill caught my attention for its cute wordplay. On the left, a red brick building, the historic Chincoteague Fire Department flanked the two-lane road. Just beyond it was the tiny Island Theater. Its old-fashioned marquee, decorated with a thick-maned rearing palomino pinto, advertised daily showings of *Misty* and a Thursday night screening of *National Velvet*. I clearly had a lot to fit in this week.

The day before, just outside of Middleburg, Virginia, in a grass parking area filled with trucks and horse trailers, I met the first Chincoteague Pony of my life: a coal black mare with four white hooves named Cricket. The mare, who loves to foxhunt, was a 2001 Pony Penning alumna.

Katrina Balding Bills leases the mare from a former college classmate who is living abroad. Katrina's adolescent daughter had just completed a judged pleasure ride on Cricket. I was told Cricket's owner has pictures of her as a filly swimming the channel and trotting down Main Street with the herd en route to the Chincoteague Carnival Grounds.

As we talked about my upcoming island trip, Katrina said she attended Pony Penning five years earlier. She said all the food trucks were delicious and all the foals she saw were "smart, brave, athletic and straight-legged."

Maybe the allure of the ponies wasn't solely to recreate a childhood dream from the Misty books, I thought. That observation flew out the window with her next revelation. "I read *San Domingo: Medicine Hat Stallion* to my son when he was little, and after that, he wanted one." Pintos with the rare markings in which the ears and poll wear a splash of color like a hat were thought to keep their riders safe from injury, death and draw out game while hunting. Katrina said, "I found our medicine hat gelding Odie for sale on Facebook."

A book Marguerite wrote over fifty years ago influenced this family's horse shopping selection!

Continuing down Main Street on the right I saw a bronze statue of a playful foal version of Misty, tail flicked up, frolics with a duck flapping its wings. A shop named Decoys Decoys Decoys lay beyond it. I passed a couple seafood restaurants and pulled into the parking lot of my hotel, realizing just how close to the water it was. The air conditioning of the lobby met me at the door, blocking out the humidity I plodded through from car to entry. My introductory pass through the charming town over, I was ready to relax. The next morning I would ponder ponies and hopefully meet some of their superfans.

***

Sunday, my first full day on Chincoteague, I drove to Chincoteague National Wildlife Refuge, on Assateague, the larger barrier island. Much like my one time in Yellowstone National Park when cars pulled over to the side of the road it signaled wildlife such as a bear or bison up ahead, cars were pulled over for ponies. The southern herd of about thirty mares, stallions and adorable foals milled about in a corral, munching on hay and grazing as pony admirers paused by the double fence line. I spied the ridiculously good-looking stallion Riptide, the one whose Facebook Group I had joined. He was drinking from a Rubbermaid water trough, but I don't think he saw me as both eyes were covered with his thick flaxen forelock. A palomino pinto mare with a star reminiscent of the lightning bolt emoji, who, according to my Chincoteague Pony names app, was Little Miss Sunshine, grazed close to the inner fence and her Mini Me filly.

A sign with a galloping bay pinto labeled as Henry's Hidalgo said, "Do not ever feed the ponies! You can kill them! Horses and ponies have weird digestive systems that are not like people, cats or dogs. They can COLIC or FOUNDER which causes great PAIN and even DEATH if they eat things that don't agree with their tummies. Too much green grass, grains (like corn, sweet feed), treats like apples, carrots or human food can be deadly ... Chincoteague ponies have centuries of evolving and adapting to a salt marsh/barrier island environment and giving them anything out of their ordinary diet can make them very sick ... If you see a sign we mean it! If you see a pony don't feed it! Thank you, CVFD." I appreciated the firm and thorough explanation. No wonder there was an inner and outer fence line.

The wild ponies seemed anything but. Even the foals, who I guessed had never been this close to humans before, calmly nursed, napped or taste tested grass and hay. Despite cars driving slowly past the corral, people pointing at them, and even a photographer on a step stool—the ponies ate, drank and relaxed. They appeared completely unbothered as though we weren't gawking at them. They were more petite than I had envisioned them, appearing perfectly proportioned, like shrunken horses.

After I had taken several photos of the herd, I drove to Tom's Cove. In the book *Sea Star: Orphan of Chincoteague,* the orphan foal Sea Star was discovered here next to his lifeless mother. I arrived at the Visitor's Center just in time for a birdwatching talk. "Summers are for pony people and spring and fall are for bird people because you can see their migration," said Audrey, the twenty-something park ranger She handed me binoculars and pointed out snowy egrets and sandpipers. Audrey stated she loved Virginia, and it was clear she thoroughly loved her job, as she spouted off fun facts and interesting details such as asking me if I'd noticed the ponies' bellies look a little bloated. I said I had. She explained it was due to the salty cordgrass which makes up eighty percent of their diet.

Assateague Island straddles both Maryland and Virginia, and a boundary fence divides the territory. Audrey elaborated on the differences in the herd management between the Chincoteague Pony herds. Misty's extended family, the Virginia herd, is technically fenced in on two vast ranges. It's for the ponies' protection so they don't go to the beach or get on the roads. The Maryland herd's management policy is hands-off. Sadly, ponies get hit by cars once in a while, but more frequently the Maryland ponies get too close to beach goers. I've seen YouTube videos of Maryland's ponies raiding sunbathers' picnics on the shore, but really, who can blame them? It's their home, and the humans are guests.

Although not a horse person herself, Audrey grew up reading the Misty books and came to see the ponies in person on Assateague when she was a little girl. When I asked her what draws people, she said, "It's the romantic notion that you could love and ride a wild pony."

During my earlier interview with Darcy, the photographer, she highlighted what I should do every day of Pony Penning Week. I typed a long itinerary to maximize the experience. She highly recommended the pre-dawn pony beach walk when the northern herd is guided by the Saltwater Cowboys into a corral next to their southern herd pony brethren.

"Get to the refuge at 5 a.m. Park at the beach parking lot, walk north and watch the sun come up. It's something everybody should see once in their life. They'll come by you around 6:30 a.m. Enjoy the beach and wait until traffic clears." I told her how much I hated traffic. She confessed she was originally from a big city too, and when people spoke of the traffic jams, it was not really that bad.

That night I set my alarm for 3:30 a.m. in order to be ready for the Monday morning Assateague beach walk. I thought back to other times I was up at 3 or 4 a.m. when I foxhunted or had to warm up at a horse show. This is what we horse-crazy people do—early morning wakeups.

The next morning, my excitement mounted as I drove through a cloak of blackness the five miles from my hotel to the beach. The arm for the entrance gate to Chincoteague National Wildlife Refuge was up. When I arrived in the parking lot, park rangers were directing vehicles where to park. As I fumbled around in the back of the rental car digging for my beach towel, baseball cap and water bottle, I noticed a woman in the car next to me doing the same thing. We set out for the beach at the same time and struck up a friendly conversation. I learned she had driven from Atlanta by herself to see the ponies. A friend had told her about the pony roundup and auction and because she thought it sounded fun, she drove roughly eleven hours to see it for herself.

Under a sliver of moon, we walked and talked the distance to the beach. We planted ourselves in the sand behind a rope meant to be a boundary keeping the hundreds, possibly thousands, of other pony fans at a safe distance from the impending action. My new friend Jing shared how she was born in China and moved to the United States in her twenties, and had just recently retired as a mechanical engineer. She loved to travel and was passionate about skiing. With a wide smile Jing gushed, "Last year I spent forty days skiing. I think I would like to ride a horse. I love going fast!" When her daughter was little, she would take her to riding lessons when they lived in upstate New York.

As I told her about my horse Knight with the rhythmic rushing and retreating of the Atlantic providing atmosphere, a soft, narrow band of orange rose parallel to the water. I shared how I had reserved a kayak to watch the Wednesday Pony Swim and she decided she wanted to do that too. I gave Jing the name of the rental company and said we could go out together on Wednesday and observe the ponies up close.

The sky slowly morphed from black into shades of salmon and smoky blue. Silhouettes of other pony seekers carrying lawn chairs and beach blankets headed north, seeking their best viewing spots. At 6 a.m. a fiery coral sun peeked above the horizon, and many of us began taking photos of the Pony Beach Walk warm-up act—sunrise over the Atlantic.

As we waited, I chatted with a woman seated in the sand on my left who had recently retired and moved to Chincoteague. She asked me if I had met any of the Saltwater Cowboys. When I said no, she said all the people working at the carnival would be Saltwater Cowboys, and explained how nobody gets paid and it's as though the volunteer firefighters have day jobs in order to support their passion—being a volunteer firefighter. She shared that all longtime island residents have at least one family member who is in the volunteer fire company, and when you hear the fire alarm go off and see firefighters rush out, it's usually a pony in distress. In winter, the firefighters drop off large round bales of hay for the ponies, and if the herd's water holes get too low, they will top off the holes with their fire hoses. I was impressed at the fire company's level of devotion to the herd.

I asked her if she knew anyone personally who owns a Chincoteague Pony, and she said she had a friend with one, "a very expensive lawn ornament." The friend's daughter also wanted a Chincoteague Pony foal and worked the last two years to raise money for the foal auction. She found a job parking cars before she was even sixteen. I was told the girl's grandmother "doesn't have much time left," and planned to match her granddaughter's funds. The teen had raised $6,000 and had a chance to buy a car, but instead she continued to drive her 1982 Datsun that was in such bad shape, "you can hear it from about four miles away."

As I listened to the stories of the newish Chincoteague resident, I both admired and related to this teen's commitment to a horse dream. I recycled aluminum cans, squirreled away birthday and Christmas money from my grandparents and got my first job in our small-town grocery store at fourteen, to save for a horse.

Seated behind us were a father and daughter from Pittsburgh. Lizzie, the adult daughter was a self-professed Misty fanatic, Breyer horse collector, and model horse show judge. When I told her I was writing a book about Misty and Marguerite, she pulled out her phone and showed me a picture of her Misty Breyer model horse on the steps of the Beebe house, art imitating life from 1962 when Misty weathered out the Ash Wednesday Storm in the kitchen.

"When I was here last time, we did the Step Through Time Tours and went to the Beebe Ranch and I had Billy Beebe sign Misty. We stayed at Miss Molly's Inn where Marguerite stayed when she wrote Misty. You have to go there!"

When I told her my plan to kayak to watch the pony swim, she said she wanted to join in with her boyfriend's kayak that they happened to bring along. She had never kayaked before. We exchanged phone numbers via text in order to touch base later. After her first and last name, she texted the title "Misty Girl."

The people near us started standing up, facing north, and we followed suit. I strained to see a great moving mass heading toward us. It was 6:54. As the mass drew near, I could distinguish three baseball-cap-wearing Saltwater Cowboys leading the cavalcade. They came loping on a palomino, dapple gray, and bay. As horses and riders shot past us, cheers rose above the waves and wind. Next, two four-wheelers followed along with a dozen or so more Saltwater Cowboys. Behind them, a giant cluster of riderless ponies—pintos, bays, palominos and chestnuts—walked and trotted along. The Chincoteague Ponies knew the routine.

Shouts of "Hey! Hey! Hey!" and "Yah!" and intermittent shrill whinnies rang above the tidal swell. More Saltwater Cowboys rode along the beach side of the herd; on the opposite side of the procession, the ocean itself served as a boundary. I looked for the foals, but they were hard to see, sticking close to the sides of their mothers.

A brown and white pinto, ears pricked forward, trotted ahead of the throng, breaking away ankle-deep into the ocean. A cowboy turned his horse back to cut him off—he was at least one hundred feet away—and the pony pivoted on his haunches, splashing back toward the end of the line. I found out later that the pony was Norm, Darcy's favorite. Norm, whose pedigree name is Norman Rockwell Giddings, was not attempting to evade the roundup. As a young stallion without his own band of mares, he is a low man in the herd hierarchy. His ocean scamper was an attempt to stay away from the drama of herd dynamics of the older stallions and mares who bully him with their teeth and hooves.

I quickly snapped a selfie with the stream of ponies behind me, the white fluff of breaking waves behind them. And just like that, in the span of two minutes, the herd had passed. A man with a backpack ran down the beach behind them. As I pivoted to watch the ponies until I couldn't see them anymore, I realized spectators were standing five to six people deep behind the boundary rope.

The march of the herd happened fast, but it was worth it: getting up early, finding my way through the dark parking lot and plopping down amid a bunch of people I didn't know. The anticipation, excitement, expectancy and seeing the storybook ponies filled me with joy.

After waiting out the traffic, I drove back to the pony corrals where I met Rebekah Hart and Amanda Geci, founders of the International Chincoteague Pony Association and Registry. Rebekah lives on a family farm in Minnesota with her herd of eight Chincoteague ponies, one of them a Misty descendent stallion. She's a graphic designer and started a company with her sister that uses drones to spray farmers' crops. Amanda is an Army civilian logistician and walking encyclopedia of all things Chincoteague Pony. Amanda has been attending Pony Penning Week since the 1990s, and has a Chincoteague Pony of her own in Alabama. Her plan is to retire in twelve years, get a camper, and leave it at the campground on the island. She wants to be near the ponies during the good weather months and winter in Alabama.

Amanda knows all the ponies by name and can cite sires and dams going back several generations. I asked her how she learned all the ponies' names and family trees.

"I've been coming to Pony Penning for twenty-seven years. During the winter, I go on YouTube and find random videos from old news reports or educational films where there is a clip about Chincoteague Ponies and I will ID them from that."

We spoke as we watched the northern herd and southern herd mill about inside their respective corrals. Two stallions groomed each other, muzzle to withers. I couldn't believe my eyes. I marveled at herd behavior that I had never witnessed before. The day before, I had seen Riptide mount a mare, and when he was done, a foal strolled up to him and sniffed his tail. The stallion did nothing.

"Usually stallions are pretty cool until they're given a reason not to be," Amanda explained.

We started discussing stallions, and she told me Don Leonard and Hoppy are the studs that would tend to have foals that are a bit taller. "There's one cantankerous old stallion who swims his band out to Pope's Island. It's nearby and small, so they don't have to compete for grazing. He really knows how to take care of his women," she chuckled.

I asked Amanda what she thought motivated people to get a pony.

"Sometimes it's an impulse purchase or a souvenir. It's not unusual for someone to have a ten-year-old pony living in their backyard, and they have done nothing with it. We hope to provide more resources on training. You have to spend time with them when they're young, not underestimate being around them at the very beginning. You should talk to Kendy Allen. She has the Chincoteague Pony Drill Team." I learned Kendy is just one trainer out of a handful who will start new pony owners' auction foals, acclimating the youngsters to domesticated life.

Rebekah said they have plans for the International Chincoteague Pony Association and Registry to give out awards and incentives for owners to get the ponies properly trained. The registry wants to provide support and education. Goodbye expensive lawn ornaments. Marguerite would be proud.

***

The next morning, I walked from the Fairfield Inn to Robert Reed Waterfront Park to meet up with a Chincoteague tour group. Two effervescent, tank-top wearing women with graying hair asked me to take their picture as they posted next to the bronze Misty statue.

The sisters from Virginia, not horse people, were Pony Penning Week first timers, too. I asked what made them decide to come to Chincoteague.

"Misty!" they chorused. Their second-grade teacher had read *Misty of Chincoteague* to the class.

I was amazed. How does Marguerite's story that we were introduced to in childhood still hold sway over us as adults, decades later?

I understood my connection to the story as a very horse-centric person with geographic ties to Marguerite's home at Mole Meadow. I often thought how cool it was that I rode horses along the same pathways Marguerite had ridden decades earlier, and how the show grounds at which I once earned a reserve champion in hunters with my heart horse was down the street from her little horse farm. My reason for fangirling was obvious. But the sisters weren't horse crazy, nor was Jing. In fact, Jing had never even heard of the Misty story, but she heard of the ponies. They were enough to beckon her to witness their swim to the beautiful land across the water, in a roundup tradition that has occurred annually since 1924.

The tour guide began, "If you're not familiar with *Misty of Chincoteague*, it's a dream of a story."

She's exactly right. I couldn't have said it better myself.

16

SWIMMING PONIES AND WINNING PONIES

Five flashy pintos and a palomino with a white mohawk mane trotted around the perimeter of KerKaKen Acres riding arena, about a thirty-five-minute drive from Chincoteague on the Virginia mainland. The teens riding the Chincoteague Ponies bareback grinned from under their helmets, feet dangling well past their ponies' sides. "Ain't No Mountain High Enough" blared through a loudspeaker as the girls played a mounted game reminiscent of musical chairs. It was the Chincoteague Pony Drill Team open house for Pony Penning Week, and I leaned against the top rail of the arena fencing. Amanda of the pony registry stood next to me. Several families, some with tykes and some with tweens, stood beyond her.

The music stopped. Riders leaped off their ponies' left sides, bolted around them, and swung up on the right. A female announcer from an elevated stand encouraged them, "Go! Come on, come on, come on!"

The palomino rider, unable to remount before the others did, was out. The teen led the gelding who I later learned was Misty's great-great grand foal, Misty's Sunfire, to the middle of the arena. The pony, who had one blue eye and one brown eye, placed his front hooves on a mounting block-sized platform painted with gold stars, striking Misty's signature pose. When the song started again, the remaining riders cantered. The game progressed, round after round, until a winner was declared.

The most entertaining segment of the open house was a fundraising-free-for-all. The ground rules were there were basically no rules, as spectators along the arena held out cash—donations for the drill team. In the center of the ring were buckets, one per rider. The goal was for each rider to fill her bucket with as many bills as possible. When the announcer shouted, "Go!" ponies dashed madly in every direction. I held up a couple of dollars which were snatched away by a zealous equestrian and galloped off to a bucket. The enthusiasm of the teens in this friendly competition was so contagious, I reached into my purse and pulled out more singles. We railbirds laughed at the girls' cutthroat riding and G-rated trash talk. The Chincoteague breed's handiness and unflappable nature dazzled me.

Next up was a cakewalk, similar to musical chairs, but without chairs. Participants from the crowd strolled around the arena and paused when the music stopped. Rebekah, Amanda's registry colleague, and her mom urged me to join them. The overcast sky began to drizzle, but that didn't dampen the cheerful vibe. The cakewalk entry fee was a dollar, and the prize was a Misty's Twilight Breyer model horse signed by Maureen Beebe.

I meandered around the arena as music played, thinking about the simplicity of this fun and the welcoming pony posse. I had arrived on the island alone just a few days earlier, not knowing a soul. A few weeks earlier I had a phone interview with Rebekah, and during our initial phone call she invited me to come to their farm, Hart's Island Pony Ranch, to meet and ride her ponies! I was floored that a person I had never met, who had no idea of my riding abilities, or even if I was a decent human, would extend such a generous offer to a stranger.

Rebekah, her mom, and Amanda welcomed me into the fold. Earlier I stopped at the refreshments table and bought my once-a-year hotdog (reserved for special events such as baseball games and now Pony Penning Week). The volunteer, a drill team girl's mom, threw in a homemade cookie for free.

I didn't win the cakewalk model horse prize, but I accrued more steps toward my daily count, and I felt a part of something positive and welcoming. Although I've been a horse girl for most of my life, there have been times I've felt like an outsider. When I was about the age of the girls riding the drill team ponies, a riding instructor in Wayne—the village where Marguerite and Misty lived—told me I couldn't join Pony Club because I didn't own Jim Dandy, the horse I was borrowing from our family friend. I was devastated.

As an adult, during my four-year horse hiatus after my heart horse of sixteen years had colicked and died, I was overjoyed to finally re-enter the horse world by taking riding lessons. Over a series of weeks, I sent several emails and left voicemails for trainers. I stated my horse experience and that I was going to be horse-shopping within the next several months. Only one trainer replied.

I'm now well beyond the age of being chosen for teams on the playground, but the Chincoteague Pony crowd made this middle-aged Thoroughbred fan feel as though I already belonged.

After the cakewalk, Amanda strolled with me over to the announcer's booth to introduce me to Kendy Allen, the founder of the Chincoteague Pony Drill Team, owner of Misty III and the farm hosting this event. The taffy and pearl pinto known as M3 strongly resembles the pony Marguerite and generations of readers fell for. Earlier I'd had my picture taken with the mare, as though she were a celebrity. I didn't want to take up much of Kendy's time while she was in the middle of hosting the open house. Amanda got Kendy's attention and introduced me as a writer working on a book about Marguerite Henry. She smiled down from the announcer's booth.

"Marguerite Henry was my friend. When my daughter was little, Marguerite would call from California—it was late here—around 11 o'clock. I would wake my daughter up to talk to her. I would hear giggles from the other room while they talked. It warmed my heart."

I wondered if Marguerite had forgotten about the time difference between coasts—she would have been in her late eighties—or if she was so in her creative zone that time was immaterial.

I later found out how Kendy, a librarian from the East Coast, connected with her favorite author and became friends. Kendy had read all the Marguerite Henry books as a child and as an adult, lived a life immersed in horses, writing, and books (she's written seven books about Chincoteague Ponies). Her family of six had Quarter Horses and a Shetland; Kendy, her husband and kids all rode. Kendy had been to Chincoteague

Island several times during her thirty-eight years as a 4-H leader, traveling with groups of boys and girls, showing them how ponies don't need to be pampered animals in a barn. Together they would observe the wild herd on Assateague as a case in point.

One family vacation on the island changed everything. In 1988, Kendy's family went to the island's miniature pony farm, and the owner showed them a foal for sale. Kendy was not interested. They had come to the island for vacation, not horse shopping; besides, they already had horses at home. Next, the farm owner told Kendy he had been thinking about selling Misty II. That grabbed her attention. The thirteen-year-old chestnut pinto mare with the famous grand dam had earned a reputation as a rogue. She had never even been trained to ride. Tourists would visit the farm, reach over the stall door and pluck strands from her mane.

"She was the most beautiful pony I had ever seen, and my husband said we should buy her, and those magic words, 'I'll pay for it.'"

Despite her lack of training, the mare loaded into the trailer like a pro, and was delivered to the Allens' farm, then located in Pennsylvania, for a new beginning. "She was one of the best ponies I've ever had in my life." Misty II became a hunter pony champion and all of Kendy's children eventually rode her. Kendy decided to write a letter to Marguerite.

"My letter said, 'You might like to know we still love Misty, and we have one of her offspring, and she is a super pony.' One day—it was the time of day with four kids around, everything would unravel—I was getting supper ready before my husband came home from work. The phone rang, and this very sweet voice asked, 'Can I speak to Kendy Allen?'" It was Marguerite.

"This is *somebody*, and here we were on a rinky-dink, rainy roof farm in Lancaster County Pennsylvania, but she called back and our friendship just grew."

Although they never met in person, the two women on opposite coasts from different generations, united in their love for ponies, books and children, formed a lasting bond through letters and phone calls. Today Kendy owns one of the largest herds of Chincoteague Ponies, save for the Chincoteague Volunteer Fire Company. Her positive experience with the formerly rogue Misty II makes her a passionate advocate for the breed. Misty II demonstrated intelligence and a willingness to please—qualities she believes make the breed a great choice for anyone. She also views their size as perfect for children moving up from a small pony who are not yet ready for a horse.

Kendy and family eventually moved from their farm in Pennsylvania to a farm in Virginia because of the ponies. She managed the Chincoteague Pony Centre for years. Today she is both preserving the Misty line and providing opportunities for young people to meet, love, and ride the ponies, even if they can't have a pony of their own. During the 2022 Christmas season, the Chincoteague Pony Drill Team appeared in nine parades in sixteen days with a lineup of Misty's Thunderstorm, Misty's Sunfire, Misty's Irish Mist and Misty's Heart of the Storm to spread holiday cheer and act as ambassadors for their breed.

***

My first day on Assateague Island, the Sunday before Pony Penning, I spotted a sign for a hiking trail and I thought it would be fun to take in more flora and fauna beyond the ponies. I had already doused myself in mosquito repellent and wore a long sleeve shirt and cropped athleisure pants. My body was mostly covered. Only fifty feet into my woodsy hike, an unmistakable and annoying high-pitched sound buzzed near my left ear. Mosquitoes love me. I waved my hands around my head, trying to protect my face. Itchy prickles zinged my ankles, forcing me to turn around and jog-walk back to my rental car, arms flailing. Later, red welts formed on my ankles. I couldn't stop myself from scratching, even though I know you're not supposed to. The island mosquitoes are next level. I never did hike on Assateague that week.

As I prepared for the Wednesday early-morning Pony Penning Day swim, I armed myself with mosquito repellent, throwing it into the bag I had already packed with sunscreen, bottled water, a couple of granola bars and a waterproof case for my iPhone. Beyond defeating my tiny blood-sucking foes, three things concerned me about the pony swim: (1) The rainy forecast. I hate being cold. But a local assured me, even if it rained, I would not be cold. (2) Paddling a small kayak in an area with motor boats nearby; and (3) Having the urge to use the bathroom while stationed in the kayak awaiting the ponies. I pushed the second fear out of my mind and practiced self-control for number three by only drinking a few sips of my hotel-room coffee.

I met Jing at the kayak rental dock. The owners, a mother and daughter team, told me the people in boats would have anchored for their prime viewing spots the day before, overnighting on the boats. They set me up with a red kayak and gave me a push off the dock. The sky, a kaleidoscope of grays and blues with peekaboo sun rays emerging from the clouds, reflected on the glassy waterway.

Jing and I dipped our paddles into the water and caught up on our activities since meeting at the Monday beach walk. It had been only two days earlier, but it felt like a month had elapsed. We cruised past single and double-story homes with docks and an "island" of black mussel shells clumped together. A pontoon boat's low rumble signaled its approach and passed us on the right. A man on board waved at us. In the distance, the red and white Assateague lighthouse pointed into the sky, rising above the thick woods.

After about twenty minutes of paddling, the water opened up into a wide space. A flotilla of pontoon boats, one of them with a tiki bar and an American flag, had established their viewing spots. A long boundary of PVC pylons connected with a garland of colorful pennants lay before us demarcating the line behind which all the watercraft had to remain. We glided over to the party zone and tied our kayaks to the pennant line. I had a front-row seat to where the pony swim lane action would happen!

It was about 7 a.m. and the ponies would arrive during slack tide, a brief window with no current, which would end up being around 9 a.m. Under normal circumstances, a two-hour wait for anything would seem unbearable, but the history and charm of the setting, plus the energy of my fellow spectators, gave it a sense of magic. It reminded me of the times I had seen the Tournament of Roses Parade in person, held annually on New Year's Day. The parade experience was such a departure from everyday life. The celebration started in the late 1800s when Midwesterners who had newly settled in Pasadena, California, wanted to show off the sunshine, citrus and brilliant January flower blooms to their families hunkered down in snow. They longed to display the paradise they had found to the world beyond the San Gabriel Valley. Despite the mosquitoes and intense humidity, both rugged Assateague and inhabited Chincoteague evoked a different type of paradise—one of sea-kissed natural beauty and small-town America.

I read an account stating when Marguerite Henry and Wesley Dennis attended the pony swim in 1946 to do their homework for writing and illustrating *Misty*, they separated, both with cameras, to take pictures from two different perspectives. When the swim was over, they met up and neither of them had taken a single photo. Both author and illustrator were too immersed in the unfolding drama. Their research oversight clearly did not impact the quality of the story. I knew I needed to document this momentous event, so my iPhone was at the ready, but I wanted to observe the nuances of ponies sloshing through the salty water before my eyes, firsthand.

While waiting for the big moment, I chatted with my kayak neighbors. A mother and daughter from Boston who had been to the pony swim once before were next to me on one side. The mother, a fine art photographer who does ranch riding in her surprisingly non-western location, wore a straw cowboy hat and a visible layer of sunscreen. She excused herself from the conversation, stating the camera she had with her was not in her "first string." She needed to practice with it to make sure she was ready for the ponies.

I surveyed the crowd that had formed behind me. Near a green canoe, a dad stood on a sandbar playing with two little kids wearing arm floaties. An Amish family dressed in dark garb sat together in a silver fishing boat.

Another nearby kayaker told me Marguerite Henry is the reason she owns horses today. She owns a Percheron and Dutch Harness Horse, and when she's not driving her horses, she travels with a group of friends on riding vacations around the world. She's already been on an African riding safari and to Ireland and Peru, and her next trip is to Egypt. I asked her if she would be picking up a pony at the auction.

"No, my husband watched me leave to make sure I didn't go down the driveway with my truck and trailer."

The clouds gave way to the sun, and a mass of horses and ponies appeared in the distance. Shouts of "Hey! Hey! Hey!" rang out as legions of legs sloshed through the channel. The Saltwater Cowboys, in the lead on horseback, walked through water. They walked and walked and walked.

Maybe it's not really a swim, but just a walk through deep water. A pony "swim" sounds more romantic for tourists.

Just as I was preparing myself for disappointment, the lead cowboy's horse was chest-deep in the water and soon after, all the cowboys' horses' heads paralleled the water's surface, nostrils peeking above the surf.

In small groups, the wild ponies began swimming too. "Yay, ponies!" I burst out as though my cheer would lend them vigor. I videoed the splashing and paddling on my iPhone, tucked in its waterproof case. By this time, the sun was so bright I couldn't tell if I was capturing anything on the video, torn between trying to watch the event in real time and trying to preserve it to watch for months, maybe years to come.

"That one looks like Misty over there!" I exclaimed to no one in particular, as my kayak swayed while the ponies churned seemingly thirty feet away from me. I'm a terrible judge of proximity, but I was close enough to see a couple of petite foal heads resting on their mothers' rumps, catching a bit of a ride. I heard the rhythmic purrs of their exhales as they swam right past me. The swim itself lasted briefly—like a horse race, like the beach walk procession from two days earlier—but the excitement lingered. Stallions, mares, and foals reached the muddy bank of Chincoteague where they rested for about an hour before being driven down the street to the carnival grounds. I missed the thirty-minute pony parade along Main Street, but I would not have traded my front row kayak seat and meeting fellow pony fans for anything.

As Jing and I began paddling back to the dock, a young woman in a kayak asked if one of us could take her picture. During a bit of chitchat with Bailee, I discovered she'd driven by herself, fourteen hours from Illinois after a friend with whom she volunteered on weekends at a racetrack told her about the pony swim. She said the event sounded amazing, so she asked off work and camped in her truck. I remarked we could have road tripped together, had we only known each other. She had not heard of Marguerite nor Misty, but like Jing, the very idea of the wild ponies called to her, beckoning her to their marshy home.

***

"We missed you guys," the auctioneer spoke into his microphone from his perch at the first in-person Pony Penning foal auction since the pandemic (it had been held online in 2020 and 2021). The two previous years' auctions held online broke all prior sales records.

It was now Thursday of Pony Penning Week, and the auctioneer spelled out the ground rules for the sale. "Foals numbered forty-three through fifty-seven will not be available to go home until August twenty-seventh, and fifty-five on up not until October first. We will accept cash, MasterCard or Visa, but by using a credit card, there's a three percent convenience fee. You have no excuse not to buy a pony," he half-joked. I was glad to hear some of the younger foals, not ready to be weaned, could stay with their dams for several more weeks.

A Chincoteague Pony Drill Team rider on a chestnut pinto pony held an American flag, leading the team around the foal pen to an instrumental version of *The Star-Spangled Banner*. Next, the auctioneer instructed, "Everybody raise your hand. When you want to bid, leave it there." A lively mood permeated the carnival grounds and potential pony buyers and people there like me, just for the spectacle, squeezed in their lawn chairs, hats and sunglasses, hoping for a coveted spot under a sun canopy.

To my surprise, the foals weren't the only items being auctioned to raise funds for the Chincoteague Volunteer Fire Company. A tiny crocheted baby firefighter outfit was on the block, and later Maureen Beebe's saddle. The fifty or sixty-year-old Stubben sold for $7,400.

The preliminaries over, foal number one, a bay pinto filly with a blaze, entered the ring. Three beefy volunteer firefighters accompanied the filly, two of whom hugged her from chest to tail as was she half-carried and half-walked on spindly legs around the ring. Midway through the auctioneer's rhythmical word whirring, the filly dashed sideways, attempting to evade her handlers. The men followed her, maintaining contact. The winning bid belonged to an online bidder at $2,750. When the auctioneer cried, "Sold!" the crowd erupted with applause.

When bidding started for a palomino pinto filly, a little girl with braids and a face painted from the carnival raised her hand. After some back and forth with other bidders, and one more hand raise, the auctioneer boomed, "Sold!" The little girl had won. Next to her, a gray-haired woman's face lit up. The two got up and walked toward the auction booth to pay for the pony. The child's pink T-shirt read, "Nana said I could."

A pinto filly with blue eyes and a wide blaze running the length of her dark brown head arrested my attention. A piece of rope like a necklace bore tag number twelve, parting her vertical brown and white mane. Besides her beauty, the auctioneer said she was a Misty descendant. He shared this information for all the foals who were members of Misty's family tree. I snapped a couple of photos on my iPhone of the filly, who I later learned is the daughter of Riptide, the popular stallion with a Facebook fan page. An online bidder won the pony with a bid of $9,000.

The previous day, I stopped by the carnival grounds to see the ponies congregated in the corral after the pony swim. My heart leaped when an inquisitive bay pinto foal, with a dash of white on its nose ambled over to me. I squatted down and snapped a photo through the chain-link fence. He or she was so close I could make out the old man fuzz inside its pricked ears. I tried to pick out a favorite, but it was impossible because they were all so cute. Some foals had red spray paint on their sides, some green, and some had no paint. The red meant they were buybacks, the green too young to be separated from their mothers, and no paint meant they were good to go. They all had a number tag on their hips.

A woman next to me wearing fashionable round sunglasses the color of an eggplant started telling me about three "very sweet" Chincoteague Ponies who were part of her ten-horse herd at home in North Carolina. She told me that her mother, elderly and in a wheelchair, was unable to make the trip. We had such a great conversation that we exchanged phone numbers. By this time I had already added several Pony Penning attendees' numbers to my contacts list: first Jing, then the Virginia sisters by the Misty statue, then Bailee, the solo kayaker from Illinois. I have never vacationed anywhere with people so eager to talk to strangers and form friendships. This subset of horse lovers stood in stark contrast to my experience being denied Pony Club membership as a girl. It made up for the unreturned phone calls from trainers and barns in Southern California when I was seeking re-entry to the horse world.

After the auction, I received a message from the North Carolina woman with the cool sunglasses. With a heart and smiley emoji, she texted, "My mom won number twelve. Misty descendant."

It didn't make sense to me—what senior with limited mobility would possibly want with a young, not just untrained, but feral foal. The more I pondered it, I think I figured it out: this pretty pony was both a link to a glorious story and a dream. Misty's blood runs through the blue-eyed filly's veins, and in this great-great-great-great grand-foal of a pony heroine now gone, delight, joy and love live on. Just for the joy, no riding required.

In *The Illustrated Marguerite Henry,* the 1980 Rand McNally release in which Marguerite shares stories about her illustrators, Charles Hillinger, a feature writer for the *Los Angeles Times* and *Washington Post*, shares in the book's introduction, "I first met Marguerite Henry in Chincoteague, Virginia, and she was not even there. I was covering Pony Penning Days on World Wide Events for the *Los Angeles Times*. Families had driven for miles not only to watch the wild ponies swim from Assateague Island to Chincoteague, but also to buy a young colt to take home. Many of the children were clutching a book and told me about their friend, *Misty of Chincoteague*, with such enthusiasm that I determined to meet the author in person."

Like Charles, I met Marguerite on Chincoteague too. But it wasn't a first meeting, as by this stage I was already well acquainted. I met her in the smiles and stories of the people who loved her and the ponies she loved as much as I did.

17

THE MISTY MYSTIQUE

Before I moved back to the Midwest from Southern California in 2021, I spent a day hanging out with my friend and her chestnut warmblood at a horse farm near Rancho Santa Fe. In her late sixties, Marguerite moved from Mole Meadow to Rancho Santa Fe, California, a town of bright bougainvillea and towering eucalyptus trees. At this point in my book research journey, I had not yet met Kendy from the drill team, Bonnie, the last illustrator, or Ed, the man who as a boy rode Misty on trails alongside Marguerite on her Morgan. I was on a mission to find people who knew Marguerite. My friend's trainer was from the area, so while she tacked up a giant gray jumper, I asked if she had ever met Marguerite or knew anyone who had.

"You know it's funny. I read all those books growing up, but I didn't know she was from around here until a few years ago."

From two crosstie spaces down, a young woman grooming a horse piped up, "My broker lives by the Marguerite Henry house. She wanted to buy it, but it wasn't on the market." She explained her broker had settled on another house, close to where the author she so admired had lived. The woman gave me a rough idea of the Henry home location, and to my surprise, I had driven past the street without even realizing it. It's a hop, skip, and a jump from the tack shop where I had my *Horses Adored and Men Endured* book signing, where two and a half years earlier I met Laura, the criminologist, who told me about Marguerite signing her copy of *Black Gold*.

She continued on, sharing that a friend of hers from San Diego horse country bought a Chincoteague Pony at the auction. Her friend's family shipped the foal all the way to California. Her friend fell in love not just with the colt, but with Chincoteague Island itself. So smitten was she that she began making monthly trips back to the island. She then moved to the island, lived in a camper and got a job. Meanwhile, back in California, her parents sold their horse property, bought a place in Virginia and joined her on the East Coast. Along the way, the former Californian met a Saltwater Cowboy and they married.

"She works on one of the boats that takes people around the island to see the wild ponies. Her name is Sydney Lynn and if you talk to her, tell her I said hi."

That conversation provided even more validation to uncover the unwritten life stories of Marguerite and her horses. If someone desired to buy the home Marguerite had lived in and another person moved three thousand miles across the country because of reading and loving her books, eventually falling for a foal and the island itself, there must be other members of an unofficial Marguerite and Misty fan club out there too.

***

The morning of the swim back—the Friday of Pony Penning week—dawned clear. The crowds had somewhat dispersed, but there were still scores of boats of all varieties anchored in the channel. A pod of dolphins cavorted in nearby waters, their shiny finned backs gliding in and out of the water. Perhaps they too were celebrating the ponies' imminent return home.

"Are you Sydney Lynn?" I asked a smiling, very pregnant woman on the boat anchored next to the one I was on, filled with spectators awaiting the pony swim back. I had been texting Sydney Lynn, the woman I had heard about from the gal grooming her horse at my friend's barn the year before, leading up to Pony Penning Week. I knew she was thirty-seven weeks pregnant with her first child, and determined to see the ponies—the stallions and the mares, now freed from their foals—splash back to Assateague.

Sporting a thick ponytail and jean shorts, Sydney Lynn, the Californian-turned-Virginian all because of a pony, invited me to her boat. I hopped from bow to bow, eager to meet the fellow Misty lover I had connected with via text. Just like meeting the other ardent Chincoteague Pony lovers, it felt like we weren't strangers at all as we shared our horse stories. During our conversation, while waiting for the slack tide, I found out she was Kendy's next-door neighbor. Small world! Getting her first Chincoteague Pony led to another, with a tale so sweet I could imagine Marguerite writing a story about it if she were still with us.

She explained that when island life on Assateague becomes too difficult for the wild ponies, they are retired to a farm on Chincoteague. One old mare, blind in one eye, had been brought to the farm with an injured leg in such terrible shape she was scheduled to be euthanized. The morning of what was supposed to be her last day, a foal stood by her side. No one knew she was pregnant. The colt was a complete surprise! Motherhood worked wonders for the mare, and over time she healed enough to rejoin the island herd. Her foal had given her something to live for.

As I pondered this miracle foal story, I thought about the power of these ponies. Just as the surprise colt gave his dam purpose, the wild herd and their domesticated brethren do the same thing: they give purpose and hope to the people who love them, whether in person or from afar. And even though I don't have a Chincoteague Pony myself, reading about them and exploring the history of the most famous of all Chincoteague Ponies and her number one fan, Marguerite, gave me a sense of purpose. They were my anchor as I charted my course after my life's recent seismic shake. Instead of feeling rejected and alone due to the death of my marriage, like the Phantom, Misty's dam when Paul released her to freedom on Assateague where she rejoined her band, I felt embraced by a community of fellow horse lovers. I felt especially understood by those who still adored Marguerite.

Sydney Lynn bought the senior mare's miracle colt directly from the fire company, and over the next few years, the mare delivered three more healthy foals. She died of natural causes in the wild on Assateague in 2021.

***

For over twenty years Matt DesJardins has been running the website MistysHeaven.com, a site that "strives for updated and accurate information on the Misty family line, as well as offering many photographs of the ponies themselves ... information to make the Misty fan happy!"

A horse crazy boy, Matt, now in his forties and a retail manager of a footwear store in Michigan, received Breyer models for his birthday and Christmas. His mom read the Black Stallion books to him. A horse farm a couple of blocks away from his house was a magnetic force; he would jaunt off to watch horses in their fields—they fascinated him. Matt eagerly read *Black Beauty* by Anna Sewell and *Summer Pony* and *Winter Pony* by Jean Slaughter Doty, but Marguerite Henry books were his all-time favorites. And it all started thanks to an elementary school reading contest when he was in third grade.

Matt's reading contest prize was a book of his choosing from his school's book fair. He had just borrowed the *Misty of Chincoteague* paperback from the library and noticed the book fair also had a copy of *Misty*. "Misty on the cover is very inviting; she's almost smiling at you. I chose it, read it, and loved it. It was a two-part thing for me, leading me to reading more of Marguerite's works. I looked in the back of the book and went back to the library for *Sea Star* and *King of the Wind*."

Matt explained, "The thing that really ignited the Misty interest was I was in the library in the non-fiction section. I saw the book *A Pictorial Life of Misty*, and I thought, 'I wonder if that's the same Misty.' I learned Misty was a real pony. It wasn't just a story. That Misty book was the origin of the website and its descendants. They're all real and they have similar weather names. Then I got the Breyer models. Misty's a pivotal part of my life."

Matt received the Misty II Breyer model horse set for his sixteenth birthday, and his curiosity was piqued about the identities of the two horses in the set with Misty II. He wrote a letter to Breyer, and Breyer forwarded the letter to Kendy Allen of the Chincoteague Pony Drill Team. Kendy wrote back to Matt, enclosing a fact sheet, and said she owned Black Mist, Twister, and Misty II—all three ponies in his set. In 1998, Matt and Kendy began regularly emailing each other, and as he created the Misty website, they forged a friendship. Meanwhile, Matt had been taking riding lessons and was working on a Welsh Pony farm. Kendy invited Matt to Chincoteague to work at the Pony Centre, and in 2006 for two weeks and the full summers of 2007-2009, Matt loaded up his car and drove from Michigan to the island and stayed at Kendy's farm. He became a drill team member and took part in the open house and demonstrations like the one I saw at KerKaKen Acres.

Because of Kendy's kindness and encouragement, Matt had the thrill of riding the ponies of his Breyer set, Black Mist and Twister. However, his favorite pony, not part of the model horse trio, was Misty's Heat Wave, Misty II's eighth known offspring, foaled on a sizzling August day.

"She was a beautiful palomino, and we just clicked. Misty ponies are so whimsical, as I discovered with Heat Wave. She was reliable, she was mellow, and she was just an amazing pony. Her Misty lineage was the icing on the cake. Did I like her because of Misty? Yes, but I liked her more because she was wonderful."

All these years later, Matt still has a picture of his favorite Misty descendant hanging on his wall. He told me anyone who has worked at

Kendy's Chincoteague Pony farm or been a part of the drill team still wishes they could rewind time and go back.

During his Chincoteague summers when he wasn't working with Kendy's ponies, Matt set off for Assateague to search for wild ponies. "There I was staying at Kendy's with a paddock full of ponies, but I would go over to the island."

The allure of the wild ponies was strong then, and it continues to hold sway over Matt. "Even though time marches on, the island and the ponies are always still there. They're still doing the roundup. Misty's descendants are still among us today."

Matt's interest in Misty's family tree drove him to learn computer coding, even though he does not consider himself very techie. "I had a friend who created a model horse website. I told her I was interested in starting up a website for Misty's family ... my friend taught me how to do html codes. She and I worked on it a bit, it was up, and then she moved on to college.

As the site was developing around 2000, Matt met Amanda Geci online, the same Amanda who co-founded the International Chincoteague Pony Association and Registry, and they bonded over their mutual pony interest. Matt asked Amanda to write for and help maintain the Misty's Heaven website. In 2006, Matt and Amanda first met in person on Chincoteague Island after they had already been pony friends for years, emailing back and forth with information and ideas for MistysHeaven.com.

Matt selected the name Misty's Heaven for his Chincoteague Pony family tree website. "I was in my late teens, trying to think of a culminating name to bring it all together. We basically made the website for us, Amanda and I joke. I go back to the website to scroll. It's like your whole family is in heaven, all the horses together in one place. Plus, if you're a diehard Misty fan, it is like heaven. I thought it was a neater way rather than saying Misty's Website."

When asked if he could explain the Misty mystique—how a pony born in the 1940s who died in the 1970s—could still exert a hold on countless fans, Matt credits the fact that the story is real and so unique. "Seeing them swim across the channel is amazing. I remember thinking, 'Wow this is it!' I remember my first swim. It's the experience, and part of that experience affects certain people. Why did I spend several years tracking down Misty descendants? I don't know. It was just so neat—a family tree. These ponies were related to this famous pony. It's the legacy and there's a certain kind of magic to it."

Maybe that's the mystique, this draw of the saltwater ponies: the magic of a story from childhood being true, or at least truth fused with a twinge of artistic license. Misty wasn't born on Assateague, a wild pony; she was foaled at the Beebe Ranch, and the Phantom, Misty's dam, was never set free. The location of Misty's setting is real. Like the rhythm of the waves lapping Assateague's shore, the pony swim happens every July as does the foal auction. (Although the swim took a two-year pandemic hiatus during 2020 and 2021).

Marguerite created a storyline that resonates today. She tapped into that innate longing for a horse of one's very own to love and care for, a best friend we can whisper our secrets to. A horse or pony will never divulge them or judge us. Some people collect paintings or sculptures or grow flowers. An equine partner is dazzling, textured art on four hooves. Their breath is sweet, their nickers kind. Our horse and pony friends model for us how to live in the moment. By riding them, we borrow their strength and swiftness. Our saddles are a gateway to something like freedom. Peace, purpose, community, beauty.

No matter how much time advances and we readers have changed and grown, our lives and responsibilities growing in complexity, or even like mine, in tragedy and loss, the Misty story, the wild ponies and their peaceful island remain the same. The wavy maned creatures nibbling on marsh grass, striding by the sea, evoke an immutable dream, a dream we can rely on.

In the book *Seabiscuit* by Lauren Hillenbrand, the small but scrappy racehorse gallops to prominence and buoys the spirits of racing fans during the Great Depression. Seabiscuit rose to fame during a time when people needed something positive to celebrate. I love an underdog story of a bay Thoroughbred gelding (as the owner of a bay Thoroughbred gelding), but what I love even more is how three people, each with a need or hurt, drew together because of a horse. Cut loose by his parents at fifteen, jockey Red Pollard lacked a family. Charles Howard, Seabiscuit's owner, lost a son. Trainer Tom Smith was living in a horse stall when he met Howard. Thanks to Seabiscuit, the men's lives entwined, creating a family with the barn as their home. All because of a horse.

Through Misty birthday parties and public appearances in the 1940s and 1950s; the formation of MistysHeaven.com and a drill team in the 1990s; and Pony Penning Week with its roundup, swim, auction and carnival attracting thousands of visitors every July (its one hundredth anniversary celebration will take place in 2025); this story of a boy and a girl and the pony they loved brings people together, united in their admiration, whether they know Marguerite's name or not. What an enduring, exquisite legacy.

***

After my conversation with Sydney Lynn, I stepped back onto the boat that had transported me to the pony swim viewing area, and plopped down at the edge of the bow, dipping my feet into the refreshing saltwater. Another woman around my age, also from the Midwest, sat next to me and we talked about our love of horses and reading. Her name was Margo. She told me she had purchased a filly at the auction, pulling out her phone to show me pictures of the red-headed cutie. My heart melted.

The water was flat and quiet, but the dozens of people on my boat and the ones lined up next to it made for cheerful background noise.

"Oh Wow! Look at them," a man behind me said as a colorful cluster of mounted Saltwater Cowboys and a now smaller Chincoteague herd walked and trotted onto a grassy area behind two condo complexes at the water's edge. This time around, the wild ponies, not the Saltwater Cowboys, led the way.

"There they go!" the man cried out. The pony swim back happened so fast, I'm glad I videoed it. I've watched the scene repeatedly, extracting details for this re-telling. It makes me appreciate Marguerite and Wesley's keen eyes all the more, remembering how they were both so dazzled by the swim they both forgot to take any photographs.

Six ponies, the Fabio-maned stallion Riptide among them, heads down, plunged into the shallows. Behind them, nose to tail, more ponies followed. Without hesitation, they surged forward chest deep, then neck deep into the channel. With ears perked and muzzles above the blue, the equine armada pumped their legs, each underwater stride drawing them closer to Assateague. The riders on horseback remained on shore. The cowboys' lead and encouragement were unnecessary: these ponies knew where they were going. Their destination was home.

A sea of blazes, stars, stripes, snips and some solid-colored faces with no white at all chugged forward as a few escort boats moved along the waterway. The boats remained at a distance far enough away to give the ponies space, but close enough to monitor their progress.

"Look at that leader, it's cutting through the water!" a man pointed out to a toddler. When the ponies swam away, our tour boat motored along, teasing a slight breeze out from the balmy air. We traveled parallel to the ponies as they reached Assateague's shore. One pony flopped down and rolled, hooves to the sky, body wriggling side to side. Kayakers held the closest positions to the herd, their pinwheeling paddles keeping pace with the trotters. From my perspective on the boat, it looked as though the kayaks were only ten feet from the soggy bodies scampering along the shore. I made a mental note to reserve a kayak for the return swim next time. I want to gaze upon the glee up close.

Cantering and splashing along the marsh's edge, the ponies passed the kayakers. Two gulls swooped in the Robin's egg sky as one pony paused to graze and another small troupe doubled back on land, regrouping according to bands.

"They're so happy!" I proclaimed to no one in particular, as I witnessed the vibrant ponies arriving home, wild and free on Assateague. I was happy too. Happy to be there and drink in their jubilation along the water's edge, where they will continue to gallop and play and swim, delighting generations to come.

The beauty of that homecoming I likely never would have known if it weren't for a writer from the Midwest who found horses a constant source of wonder.

18

A Triumphant Life

In 1971, the Henrys sold their beloved Mole Meadow and purchased a rambling ranch-style home with a pool in Rancho Santa Fe, California. Of their move, Marguerite wrote, "On a Pacific hilltop overgrown with daisies we made our home. In no way did the new Daisy Hill replace our Mole Meadow. We just expanded our hearts to fill both."

I could not find the backstory about why they left the Midwest, the land of their youth and where their siblings and their extended families remained, but I believe the Henrys chose this spot to live out their golden years not just for the mild Mediterranean climate and Pacific Coast vistas, but because it was (and still is) a community known for the two things they were most passionate about: golf for Sidney and horses for Marguerite.

The town just north of San Diego has backyard barns, miles of riding trails winding through the foothills, and several golf courses. It is minutes to Del Mar, home to the racecourse "where the surf meets the turf" founded by Bing Crosby, whose estate was about a mile away from the Henrys. Just like Mole Meadow, the Henrys' new property was two acres, and although it had no barn, their neighbors had horses. While living at Daisy Hill, Marguerite became involved in the Rancho Santa Fe Garden Club, some of her books became films, and she continued to write.

Marguerite spoke publicly of one regret in moving to Southern California: she was now an entire continent away from Misty, who was living out her golden years on Chincoteague with Ralph Beebe's family. In *A Pictorial Life Story of Misty*, Marguerite reveals her spirits rose and fell with the Misty reports received in letters from fans who visited the celebrity pony. One such postcard from a child, excited about meeting and shaking hands with the celebrity pinto mare said, "I didn't know grandmas could be so young!"

Another fan wrote, "After waiting three years, I finally saw her. Did you know she is twenty-four years old? Sad to say, you can tell she is getting older. She doesn't look like any of the pictures I saw of her except when she was little. Then she was cute and fuzzy. Now she is fuzzy again."

In 1972, Marguerite received a photo taken of Misty on the pony's twenty-sixth birthday. The then seventy-year-old author reported, "Misty looked just how I remembered her, grazing in a flower-strewn meadow." Three months later, the famous pony died in her sleep.

News of Misty's passing was broadcast around the world. Baltimore's *The Evening Sun* editor paid tribute in a feature simply titled "Misty."

The editorial ran on the same page as columns on welfare eligibility, Watergate and a political cartoon about ending the Vietnam War.

"A million or more children, in this country and abroad, have read the Misty story over the past quarter century. Many were never sure if the story were true or made up, and maybe that didn't matter. What the story brings forth, in its simple and low-key way, is the human capacity for warmth and unselfishness which is a capacity not always predominant and which, to go by the rest of the news, sometimes may not be there at all.

Misty is dead, and that's the least of it. The Misty story lives on, a tiny light in the surrounding gloom."

Ralph Beebe announced plans for fans to continue to visit Misty, and Maryland taxidermist Charles Oxenham spent a year recreating a stuffed version of the celebrated mare. Oxenham told a reporter it was "nerve-wracking" and "the hardest thing I have ever done."

Fans were divided on the matter, but Marguerite was not in favor. "All my pleas couldn't stop the drive to put Misty on permanent display instead of allowing her a well-earned rest from a lifetime of getting up on her step-stool and shaking hands and giving endless pony rides to endless lines of children and performing in plays and story hours and submitting to smothering hugs."

Sometime after the pony's passing, Marguerite received a letter from Paul Merritt, a Chincoteaguer with intentions of creating a Misty museum. He purchased the Beebe herd of Chincoteague Ponies after the death of Ralph Beebe. Merritt requested Marguerite write a book about Misty's life after the events covered in *Misty*, *Stormy, Misty's Foal* and *Sea Star*. He requested that if Marguerite's answer was going to be a no, would she at least mail him Misty pictures from *Life* and *National*

Geographic, movie stills from the Twentieth Century Fox *Misty* production, and photos from Mole Meadow? He intended to create a panorama showcasing the remarkable life of Chincoteague's most famous equine resident.

Poised to deny the request for another Misty book, Marguerite searched throughout her house in file folders, drawers and closets for Misty pictures. As she spread the photographs across the floor of her library, she ran out of space. Marguerite continued laying out pictures in the living room, down the hallway and into her bedroom. Pony photos had taken over her home! In order to avoid trampling the treasured images, Marguerite and Sid booked a room at the Rancho Santa Fe Inn to stay the night. The next morning, she organized the photos chronologically and realized Misty's life story was staring back at her, and it would make for a wonderful book.

"Suddenly the idea became intensely real; it took complete possession of me. Misty had lived for twenty-six years. For all that time she had been a part of my life. The book would be all about her adventures. I didn't mean to let myself in at all, but the paths of our lives had criss-crossed so often—that I couldn't keep it out. The story grew—as natural as Misty herself ... I found myself falling in love with Misty all over again, and it took me almost as long as it takes a mare to foal a colt to complete a story I said I would never, never write at all."

Such was the genesis of *A Pictorial Life Story of Misty*, a treasury of Misty memories. Now out of print, the book shares behind-the-scenes details about the Misty movie shot on location on Chincoteague, Misty's sheltering in the Beebe's kitchen during the deadly Ash Wednesday storm, and her post-storm appearances that had raised funds to buy back ponies previously sold at auction in other years to replenish the decimated herd, ensuring the Pony Penning tradition would continue and future generations would have Chincoteague ponies to love.

Merritt's Misty museum never came to fruition on a grand scale, but he did display the taxidermied pony, along with clusters of photos. Today, Misty and her red-and-white filly who were propelled to fame in *Stormy, Misty's Foal* are stuffed, standing at attention at the Museum of Chincoteague Island. During Pony Penning Week, I visited the museum, feeling ambivalent about seeing the dead-but-trying-to make-believe-they're-still-with-us pony crushes of my childhood. What struck me about the stuffed Misty and Stormy was, no matter how talented the taxidermist, the lifeless animals possess none of their former glory. After studying Misty, poring over photos of her for almost two years, I can say with conviction she was an unusually beautiful pony. Sun-colored dapples bloomed on her coat and blond eyelashes lined her expressive eyes. This stuffed version of the pony who trotted through millions of horse-loving children's dreams looked like the horses I drew on the margins of my junior high notebooks—simple and cartoonish.

As I read the placards near Misty and Stormy, in my peripheral vision, I noticed two women around my age enter the room. "Oh no!" one of them recoiled, retreating several steps. "I'm not ready for this," she told her friend who stood between her and the stuffed Chincoteague ponies. I completely understood her strong reaction.

Marguerite never saw the taxidermied version of the little mare she loved with all her heart, lifeless and on display in a permanent winter coat. Although she's gone, Misty is still real in our imagination to those of us who read and cherished her stories. She will always be beautiful and young, with shiny golden dapples.

***

"Book ideas have a way of exploding like a barnful of hay in a burning sun—scientists call it spontaneous combustion," Marguerite wrote in a 1967 newsletter. The author had no problem dreaming up her own stories to write. *A Pictorial Life Story of Misty* was not the only book idea pitched to her. Frequently, individuals wrote Marguerite with story ideas they hoped would inspire her to write a story for them.

During my digging through Bankers Boxes of Marguerite Henry's words and works at the University of Minnesota, I read many letters from people requesting Marguerite to write specific stories. For example, a letter from a marketer employed by a now defunct Cincinnati department store asked Marguerite to write a book about the horse farms of Kentucky. It was the early 1970s, and the retailer was about to open two new stores in Louisville and Lexington. As someone in love with Thoroughbreds and the sprawling bluegrass farms, I thought that was a stellar idea, and am disappointed Marguerite didn't bite. I would have totally devoured that book.

In 1962, the Director of Publications for Colonial Williamsburg requested that Marguerite write a book about Janus, a racehorse who had an outstanding career in Virginia. Bennet Harvey, the vice president of the Trade Publishing Division of Rand McNally, shot down that request. "At the present time Marguerite has three or four excellent ideas for books which she wants to write for us, and which we want her to write for us. Marguerite is a meticulous craftsman in her writing and it takes her a good long time to turn out one of her best-selling books. Therefore, we would hate to have her break into the schedule already established, and spend perhaps a year doing a book for another publisher."

While in the research library, I found one file folder labeled "Snowman," containing a set of three-by-five cards with handwritten notes. Marguerite's artistic cursive scrawled, "I've been looking at the pic of Snowman in my scrapbook and he's the clumsiest [the word "clumsiest" is crossed out] most beautiful lop-eared, flea-bitten gray I ... keep thinking of him." The next three-by-five card read, "Come to L.A. at studio's expense. If we agree we pay you to write a book based on Snowman. We'd agree on outline." The following card read, "MGM would pay you to write a book. He would pay me for writing the book but give me publishing rights." The last card with phrases jotted haphazardly read, "We own the rights on Snowman," and "big price for book."

Marguerite entertained the idea of writing a book about Snowman, a harness horse saved from the slaughterhouse and turned into a champion show jumper thanks to the rescue and love of Dutch horseman Harry de Leyer. For whatever reason, Marguerite never wrote the underdog horse story, but thankfully author Elizabeth Letts did, releasing *The Eighty Dollar Champion* in 2011. I finished reading the number one *New York Times* bestseller about Snowman on a Kauai beach circa 2013, my eyes welling up because I didn't want the story to end and I didn't want the big gray gelding I had fallen in love with through the pages of the book to die.

Besides fans' book suggestions, Marguerite entertained several story ideas of her own that never made it into the world: *Sophia, the Grimy Angel*; *The Two Loves of Alexander*, which was supposed to be a companion volume to *Five O'Clock Charlie*; *Muggs: International Hound*; *Sir Patrick Henry: the Bilingual Dog*, based on her standard poodle, Patrick; and *Mr. Quackenbush and His Quacker*, based on an elderly, homeless man who lived with his pet duck on Chicago's Skid Row.

Marguerite had saved a *Chicago Tribune* clipping of the dapper, suit-wearing gentleman walking his duck. Mary Alice Jones, her editor, had problems with the manuscript based on the *Tribune* story. She wrote, "The theme seems to me to have more adult appeal than child appeal. Children would probably be interested in the pet idea but if they wanted to have a duck in their rooms it would present a problem! Ducks are horribly messy in their toilet habits ... the manuscript gives opportunity for nice pictures. The question is, is the narrative too slight to be a Marguerite Henry book? Your readers normally have more to 'get their teeth into.'"

As if to soften the blow of her critique, Mary Alice added, "I can see why you wanted to write it and how it would appeal to you, sympathetic creature that you are! The lonely old man would get a hold on your heart strings."

I love that Marguerite wanted to take on the subject of poverty and homelessness in order to show children there's more to life than pony parties, birthday cake, and happy endings. Who better to engage children with the fact that sometimes life is really hard, unfair even, than a trusted author friend like Marguerite? Her attempt to give prominence and voice to a homeless man, a person on the margins of society, as a main character in a book was ahead of the times. As someone whose writing has also been rejected, it was comforting for me to realize even someone with Marguerite's talent, fame, and Newbery Medal heard no. Undaunted, she kept on writing.

My heart leaped when I opened a file and realized tucked inside was a 1980s unpublished galley proof titled *Mini-Horses*. I read it, studied the photographs, then Googled photographer Tom Nebbia, whose name appeared next to my heroine's. It turned out Tom wasn't just any photographer. He shot images for *National Geographic* for 25 years and photographed luminaries such as President John F. Kennedy, John Wayne, Billy Graham, Walt Disney and Alfred Hitchcock.

Why did this almost-finished book by such a famous writer and prominent photographer never hit library and store shelves? An accompanying file folder with over twenty pages of correspondence between Marguerite and Reading Rainbow Gazette revealed the complicated answer. Reading Rainbow Gazette intended to launch a series of thirty-two-page picture books for young readers but had no commitment from a publisher. Despite almost two years of effort, they could not secure a publisher for the author-photographer A-listers. I'm not sure why Reading Rainbow didn't just publish it on their own.

In January 1989, the mini-horse manuscript was returned to then-eighty-six-year-old Marguerite. In a post-mortem penned in April 1989, Tom Nebbia wrote, "I hold you in highest esteem, for you are obviously a person who is self taught. To learn is to grow and those who grow, do not grow old ... so here's looking at you kid."

I shot an iPhone video of the galley, thinking about the legions of Marguerite Henry fans who would be elated to see the miniature horse peering out of its stall, touching noses with an Airedale Terrier on the cover, and read about the history and characteristics of the tiny creatures on four hooves. That thought stuck with me over the following weeks, prompting me to send an email to my University of Minnesota contact to pitch the idea of them publishing *Mini-Horses*. My contact replied with sad news: "Marguerite Henry personally instructed the University of Minnesota to NOT publish any unpublished work nor allow the publication or adaptation of her books."

Today, the late author and photographer's collaboration is filed away in a cavernous underground archive near the banks of the Mississippi River. If you live or travel that way, you can set up an appointment with the university to read the galley. Ask for Marguerite Henry Collection Box 15.

***

Bonnie Shields, the illustrator who teamed up with Marguerite on what would be her last book, *Brown Sunshine of Sawdust Valley,* the story of a girl who yearned for a horse but wound up with a baby mule, grew up reading and adoring the books of Marguerite Henry. Bonnie told me Marguerite reflected that if she had children, she probably never would have written so many books.

Bonnie formed a friendship with Marguerite as they collaborated on Marguerite's *Brown Sunshine.* She would drive from her home in Bishop, California, host city of the annual Mule Days celebration, to Rancho Santa Fe and stay with the Henrys. Bonnie, Sidney and Marguerite would have indoor picnics and spend time by the pool.

Bonnie shared that at one point Marguerite stopped working for about three years to take care of an ailing Sidney, eight years her senior. Sidney Henry died in 1987; his ashes were scattered at sea. I could not locate an obituary for the man who traveled the world with Marguerite, indulged her practice of bringing a pony into the living room and whose smiles, tears or furrowed brow while reading a manuscript provided actionable feedback for his writer wife.

As I read through hundreds of papers in the Marguerite Henry Collection, I found a note crossed out that said, "Talk about Parkinsons," and handwritten notes on the backside of paperwork for an assisted living facility near Rancho Santa Fe. In a letter to Bennet and Dorothy Harvey, Marguerite wrote, "How I envy your wisdom in not moving to California or Florida or the Carolinas for your 'golden years.' Toward the last, Sid was obsessed with the yearning to go home ... there was pleading and puzzlement in his eyes when I'd say, 'But Sid, we are home.'"

Bonnie described Sidney as "a real sweet and intelligent man and Marguerite's first and best fan. Theirs was a love story as far as I could see." She said the last time she saw Sid he was "tippy" and childlike, but always smiling. "When he died, she shut down for a while, but working on our book was her escape and when she felt ready, we picked it up seriously. I have a precious little card framed in my studio from her saying she was in her writing room and working on *Brown Sunshine*—and she was HAPPY!"

Although Marguerite did not compose an obituary for her husband, disclosing to a friend that when Sid died, she felt like she was in "suspended animation," she later wrote a tender tribute to the man she had loved for sixty-four years—in the form of her own autobiography.

For years the prolific author had zero interest in writing about herself. It was the very thing she said she would "never, never, ever do!" Yet Joyce Nakamura from Gale Publishing, a persistent editor who was creating an author anthology, convinced Marguerite to do an about face on her anti-autobiography stance.

"My mind recoiled at the bumptiousness of writing a book about oneself. But there was something about Ms. Nakamura's insistence that I felt I was being directed by a Higher Source. My writing began to leap over all my objections, for to my joy, it became Sid's story. We were together again! He, through God, was directing my course as he had done all of his life. I wrote the piece to him ... the writing made me whole again."

In 1988's *Something About the Author* Marguerite wrote, "In 1987 Sidney Crocker Henry died. But no one has ever died less. He is still watching over Misty's world. What stronger proof than this? Cloudy (Misty's first grandson) and Stormy (Misty's last daughter) are getting along in years. They needed a roof over their heads to shut out the burning sun and deflect the stinging botflies and mosquitoes. Sid must have sensed such problems might arise for he left in his will money to build that roof to shade Misty's children. Life is nice and round, isn't it? As Grandma Beebe, the comforter, said to me when Grandpa Beebe died, 'No one ever dies, not a person or even a single pony. Nothing dies as long as there is the memory to enfold it and a heart to love it.'"

Following the autobiographical piece for Gale, in the fall of 1988 Marguerite began writing *Misty's Twilight*. I had not read the book published in 1992, when Marguerite was ninety. That was the same year I graduated from college, enrolled in grad school, worked two jobs and volunteered with my church's youth group. At that point I had a horse of my own, my schedule was full and my reading focused on class texts. My first exposure to *Misty's Twilight* occurred during the pandemic via audiobook.

I listened to the tale of Sandy Price, a dermatologist and single mother from Florida, who hitched an empty horse trailer to her truck and set off to Chincoteague with her children. The protagonist had adored *Misty* when she was a girl. She wanted to both introduce her son and daughter to the island ponies and bring one home to live on their farm in Ocala.

After watching the swim and going to the auction, the Price family returned home with not one Chincoteague Pony, but FOUR! Three of the ponies were foals and one was a pregnant mare named Sunshine, purchased from the Chincoteague Pony Farm. Two years later after a planned breeding, Sunshine foaled a filly sired by a Thoroughbred stud. The chestnut-and-white pinto pony named Misty's Twilight was a prodigy, excelling in cutting, jumping, and eventually dressage.

I wondered if Marguerite dreamed up an unbelievable storyline for a Misty descendant, a swan song for the pony she made famous almost a half century beforehand. Then I happened upon a *Chronicle of the Horse* article from June 1991, which had three paragraphs devoted to Misty's Twilight and her excellent scores in upper level dressage at a Florida horse show. Just like Misty, Misty's Twilight had been a real pony!

In her later years, Marguerite continued to receive fan letters from students and teachers. In reply to a teacher's invitation to come speak to her class, Marguerite declined, saying that her gait was like that of a newborn foal. In an era before video conferencing, she did, however, speak to classes via the telephone. And she continued to answer the letters she received with the help of a friend.

On September 1, 1996, *Brown Sunshine of Sawdust Valley* was published. It would be Marguerite's final work. On November 16, 1997, Marguerite died at home with her poodle Patrick Henry by her side at the age of ninety-five. A niece and nephew scattered her ashes at sea; Marguerite and Sidney were together again. Her funeral card bears a black and white portrait of a young Marguerite with a wide, lipsticked smile and dark wavy hair. It lists her dates of birth and death with the simple message, "The end is the beginning. ~ MH."

Marguerite had arranged for her Rancho Santa Fe home to be donated to Scripps Memorial Hospital Foundation. In 1998, the ranch home tucked in between eucalyptus trees sold for $750,000. Her literary estate was left to the University of Minnesota, where the royalties for her books continue to fund a children's literature professor position, supporting ongoing research and instruction for the education of young readers through stories.

I had a chance to meet via Zoom with Marek Oziewicz, Ph.D., D.Litt., professor of Literacy Education, who is the Sidney and Marguerite Henry Professor of Children's and Young Adult Literature at the University of Minnesota. Marek is not horse-obsessed, but he expressed he is the beneficiary of Marguerite's work. When I asked him if he could pinpoint what makes Marguerite Henry's work so special and enduring, he said, "I can't think of any author who writes about horses with such dedication. Marguerite was one of the voices who advocated for horses specifically, and animals in general, as creatures we need to be good to. Relating to a horse makes us better people."

I couldn't agree more.

***

Ralph Waldo Emerson defined success like this: "To laugh often and much: To win the respect of intelligent people and the affection of children, to earn the appreciation of honest critics and endure the betrayal of false friends; to appreciate beauty, to find the best in others, to leave the world a bit better whether by a healthy child, a garden patch, or a redeemed social condition; to know even one life has breathed easier because you lived. This is to have succeeded."

Marguerite Henry lived such a life, winning the affection of children, and leaving the world better through her timeless books. A 1980 note to Marguerite from a Riverside City College professor read, "Thank you for enriching my children's lives (and indeed, that of my whole family) through the years. Surely nothing is more rewarding than children and horses are. Thank you, too, for what you have meant to my children's literature classes in college. What a triumphant life yours is—bringing so much joy to others through your artistry."

Beneath the note Marguerite had written, "This note washes away all the work."

In a tribute following Marguerite's death published in *Eastern Shore News*, Kirk Mariner wrote, "No other individual of our day has had a greater impact on Chincoteague than this woman who loved children, and horses."

A successful and triumphant life indeed.

19

Marguerite My Muse

In 1946, while staying at Miss Molly's Inn on Chincoteague as she researched for *Misty*, Marguerite encountered a live seahorse. She placed the tiny creature in a glass of water by the window of her second-floor suite. When she awoke the next morning, baby seahorses were splattered on the white curtains, having spewn from their father's pouch during the night. In a 1983 note to new owners of the Victorian bed-and-breakfast, which continues to accommodate guests today, Marguerite wrote, "In embarrassment and haste I gathered father and children up and returned them to the sea. And that is why the finial to the book of Misty is decorated with a sketch of a seahorse."

Marguerite was world famous, having attained the highest level of success in her field as a Newbery author, yet she was not too proud to share her awkward moments.

Over the months, as I journeyed through time and states to get to know Marguerite, I repeatedly pondered what sets her apart from other authors. I contemplated the enduring quality of her writing and legacy.

Marguerite dedicated herself to returning fan mail, publishing a newsletter, making appearances at schools and libraries, and writing stories to delight us, even into her nineties. A model for aging well, Marguerite was passionate about her work, just like the workhorse she wrote of in *Five O'Clock Charlie*. In that story, a life of retirement in a lonely field did not suit the aged cart horse, so he leaped a fence to freedom and trotted into town where he saw his old friends and rang a bell daily at five o'clock. Charlie needed purpose and longed for connection, and so did Marguerite. She was working on her manuscript about Patrick Henry, her poodle, when she died. Marguerite never retired.

While reading through research files on one of her last projects, I stumbled across a curious blue sticky note. It had a section strategically cut out of the middle, and the bottom part of the note had been shifted upward, flush against the top. The surviving parts of the note from an editor read, "I have done my best to live up to your expectations and trust … I have handled this with as much tenderness and pride as one would a newborn filly, or a brand new baby sister! Thank you for taking me along (for the ride!)!" Marguerite had jotted a comment off to the side of the note, "I expurgated the materials. It was too generous of praise." That explained the missing section. She remained humble throughout her career.

Another facet of Marguerite's life I was surprised to learn was that she served as a hospital book lady. During the era when she wrote her 1950 release *Born to Trot* about Rosalind, a harness racing mare, Marguerite headed to a local hospital one day a week. She had just received the

Newbery Medal, yet that literary honor and her busy schedule did not keep her from visiting people and connecting with them in a time of pain. Maybe she remembered those days as a girl confined to bed with rheumatic fever when books were her companions. Perhaps that's what inspired her service. I wish I could ask her.

As of 1979, Marguerite had sold over thirteen million copies of her books. In that same year, she wrote a letter to a little girl empathizing with her yearning for a horse. "I know EXACTLY how you feel about looking at people up on a horse. They look so happy at being there that you yourself want to crawl under a rock and cry. For many years—in fact all of my school years—I lived without a horse. It wasn't until I was completely grown up and could afford a horse of my own that I was able to buy a fine black Morgan. He was worth all the waiting and longing."

No matter her age, fame or financial status, Marguerite remained, in her heart, a girl who dreamed of and lived for horses. She knew just the right things to say to those of us who were horseless, and the stories she penned were love letters to an animal, and to us.

***

I couldn't remember the last time I had ridden a pony. I was en route back to the University of Minnesota for more archival research. Rebekah, the new friend I had met on Chincoteague Island and had cakewalked with just two weeks earlier, invited me to ride one of her Chincoteague Ponies.

In February and March of that year, I had been on polo ponies taking polo lessons, but those equine athletes were technically over 14.2 hands, horse sized. Here I was, all five feet, eight and three-quarter inches of me, astride Pixie, a palomino pinto Chincoteague Pony. Surprisingly, I did not feel like a giant. Between the mare's champagne-colored ears, a lush pasture rolled out ahead of us. Beyond the fencing, row upon row of corn stalks stood tall, tassels pointing heavenward. Rebekah, Pixie's owner, rode bareback on her bay pinto mare Hope.

We walked and talked, ambling around the field with no destination in mind and no training goal. The Chincoteague Ponies momentarily gave a more elevated perspective of the world than we would have taken in from the ground on our own two feet. Hope and a higher view. Perhaps this is what my re-invention—this new, unwritten phase of my life as a Marguerite Henry historian was all about.

***

Back at the University of Minnesota, I mined Marguerite's papers for more insights on her life and work. I put headphones on like a club DJ, and placed a 78 rpm album onto a turntable. I hoped I would remember how to use a technology I hadn't touched in decades.

The record was of a 1951 radio appearance on Chicago station WLS by Marguerite and Wesley Dennis as they publicized a book signing at the department store Carson Pirie Scott on State Street. The host of the show introduced Marguerite as a dainty, feminine and enthusiastic horsewoman, and said, "Since you started to write about horses, I always think of you with perhaps a pony trailing behind or a couple of horses over in the next field."

"I like to be thought of in that way." Marguerite's voice was honey sweet.

Wesley teased her about Misty getting spoiled with too many treats, and Marguerite rose to the pony's defense. Through their lighthearted banter I sensed they enjoyed working with each other very much. Marguerite compared herself to a workhorse who goes along steadily and she described Wesley as a fleet Thoroughbred. She said they weren't a matched team, but their strengths complemented each other and they both made it to the finish line.

I wished I had a way to preserve their engaging conversation to share snippets with fellow horse friends. Why did I get such a charge out of listening to this conversation from over half a century ago? I released the question into the wilds of my mind and kept on researching.

Two days later, I was treated to an Italian dinner by Margo, another Minnesotan I befriended on Chincoteague. We met on the edge of a boat watching the pony swim back. I wanted an update on the foal she bought at the auction as well as a chance to get to know her better.

Margo and I sat in the restaurant for three hours regaling each other with tales of horses. She described the pinnacle of her horse-crazy fandom, an event that played out years earlier when she crashed the ninetieth birthday party of Triple Crown Winner Secretariat's owner, Penny Chenery. Margo bought a plane ticket to Colorado and hand-delivered a thirteen-page, homemade birthday card to the iconic horsewoman. Back when Margo was twelve, she made a book just for fun that had a self-portrait and a photograph of Penny from *Time* magazine pasted next to it. She had been a life-long fan and needed to meet Penny in person. The birthday party served that purpose, regardless of the lack of an invitation. My new pony friend didn't tell her husband of her party-crashing plan until after the fact. She said it was a life-changing experience that inspired her to be more extroverted. And even though she had always been adventurous, the Penny party took her adventurous spirit to the next level. I cracked up as she narrated the tale and wished that I had her bravado.

As I reflected on Margo's story, I realized that even though I never made a card or crashed a birthday party, our actions were similar. My research journey to discover Marguerite allowed me to both meet and honor a horsewoman I had long admired.

***

My last day in Minneapolis was supposed to be a quick day at the library. All I had left to see were four boxes containing Wesley Dennis art. I thought it would be a nice way to round out the week of research, a fitting conclusion to my Marguerite quest: examining the works of the artist who dashed out Misty, Sham, Brighty, and so many other horse characters I loved.

The prior month, before I went to Chincoteague, I stopped in Middleburg, Virginia, to see the exhibition, *Storied Friends: Marguerite Henry and Wesley Dennis* at the National Sporting Library. There, his art had been displayed behind glass. Here I was going to be able to touch the Wesley Dennis drawings with my own hands—granted, my hands would sport blue rubber archival gloves. I had arranged in essence a private viewing of the work of a master.

I grabbed a No. 2 pencil and signed in. The library room overseer said I would be located at the table closest to her desk. Uh-oh. There were no new boxes. Wesley's art, which I had scheduled to see via an email reservation three weeks prior, was not there.

I asked if she knew where the boxes were. She walked the perimeter of the room, inspecting all the carts set aside for other researchers. No

Wesley Dennis boxes. Then she disappeared to a back room. No luck. This was not how I wanted to end my week of research.

I asked if she could contact anyone else to see if they knew what was going on. In the meantime, I settled on reviewing more file folders thick with fan mail, boxes I had set aside from the day before. They held letters from students, teachers, librarians and parents. I figured I might as well make use of my time waiting for the art boxes.

I found a January 1995 letter from a reading teacher stating, "My fifth and sixth grade girls and boys thoroughly enjoyed your book *Misty of Chincoteague*. We wanted to write to let you know your popularity is not diminished since your heyday of the 50's and 60's [sic]." I'm positive that one warmed Marguerite's nonagenarian heart.

Handwritten notes from a beginner's large, plain print to artful teachers' script contained similar themes: I read your book, I like this part, I have a question, and a closing or P.S. that more often than not requested: "Please write me back." She almost always did. My mind flashed back to the Chincoteague tour guide telling our group she had met women visiting the island who had formed pen pal relationships with Marguerite Henry. For decades.

I don't know how she did it.

I loved teaching middle school, yet I felt such pressure the last few days of the school year when students jubilantly or shyly presented their yearbooks to me to sign. It was an honor knowing they wanted a message from me. I knew that was my last chance to leave an impression on them. I wanted to say good, true things, leave them with words of encouragement they could carry with them into the rest of their school years and life. A standard, "Enjoy your summer," or "I hope you enjoyed my history class," just wouldn't do. Often my hand would go a little numb on yearbook distribution day.

Once a colleague had a white wrap around his hand on the last day of school. I asked him if he had an accident, and he smirked and placed his wrist closer under my nose, showing me his "injury" was actually toilet paper wound around so he would look wounded and not have to sign yearbooks. I chuckled and thought to myself that wasn't a bad idea. But I would never do that.

It was a lot of pressure to be a good influence, encourage, challenge and ultimately love the one hundred and seventy students I was privileged to know during the course of a one hundred and eighty-five-day school year. Marguerite loved, befriended, and empathized with thousands of children around the world for over sixty years. Although she never had a child of her own, Marguerite felt a motherly, and later grandmotherly affection and concern for her fans. She was heavily invested in her work.

Marguerite once wrote about the upside-down nature of her life: how in the 1930s, most young women spent their early years caring for their children, and how when they were grown, they would dive into a career. "To Sid's and my surprise we had no chick or child of our own even though we both came from large families. So I spent my young married years in the lively pursuit of word-chasing." She wrote that in her "ungrandmotherly" years she was taking care of children she never had—her young readers who wrote her letters with "monstrous problems," from sharing their sadness at the loss of a pet or divorcing parents, and occasionally, thoughts of suicide. If a child expressed such dark thoughts to her, phone calls were made. She truly loved people and was committed to them. She imparted that gift to her readers. The fan mail kept rolling in, even after her death.

Lee Galda, the first and now retired Sidney and Marguerite Henry Professor of Children's and Young Adult Literature at the University of Minnesota, was tasked with composing a response form letter to fans who wrote Marguerite, unaware she had passed away. Lee remembers the struggle to get the tenor of that letter just right. Although she wrote books professionally throughout her academic career, Lee said writing the letter to be sent to Marguerite fans was one of the hardest things she has ever had to do.

I continued poring over letters and temporarily forgot about Wesley's art until a woman asked me which boxes I was looking for. I gave her the box numbers.

How hard could it be to pull boxes from a back room?

I carried on flipping papers from right to left, scanning the messages from decades earlier. Stationery with muted golds and greens of a palomino in a sea of prairie grass snagged my attention. I recognized the stationery as a design I had as a girl! A few minutes later, I found a letter on lined notebook paper. The careful cursive looked almost exactly like my little-girl penmanship.

Next, I felt the bumps of a Braille letter from a fan accompanied by a note stating the Braille Institute of Los Angeles transcribed Marguerite's response letter into Braille. I thought how cool it was that Marguerite valued connecting with all of her readers. She possessed a forward-thinking emphasis on inclusion and diversity. *Misty of Chincoteague* and *Brighty of the Grand Canyon* were both made into Braille books. I remembered reading in *A Pictorial Life Story of Misty* about the bittersweet day Misty boarded a trailer to return to Chincoteague, and how the last child lifted onto the pony's back for a ride was a blind girl. I reflected on her educational film, *Story of a Book*. In it, an African American girl and Asian boy paged through books, and one of the child narrators spoke with a distinct southern accent. In *Black Gold*, she wrote about the 1924 Kentucky Derby winner, bred and owned by a woman of the Osage Nation. Marguerite wanted to elevate untold stories and desired all of her fans to feel acknowledged and represented. She was ahead of the times.

Lost in uncovering and analyzing tiny clues about my muse, Marguerite, a different woman introduced herself as the curator. I knew her from my email communication but had not met her. I didn't expect to see her, as she was supposed to be on vacation. It blew me away to learn she came in to work on her day off to ensure I would get to see the Wesley Dennis materials. She offered to take me on a tour of the archive while the art was being retrieved, and I eagerly said yes.

An elevator lowered us into the literary cavern the size of two football fields. My excitement mounted as we entered a holding hallway in a double door system that reminded me of entering a butterfly farm. Instead of trying to keep butterflies in, we were trying to keep the perfect temperature and humidity inside so Marguerite and Wesley's and all the other children's authors' works, Ellis Island diaries and seventy thousand comics—to name a few collections—will be pristine for future generations of researchers. Metal shelves towered floor to ceiling in the vast archive, and one unit rose fifteen shelves high. Specially trained employees use a cherry picker to retrieve materials for researchers.

"The author Pam Muñoz Ryan wrote a letter to Marguerite Henry when she was a kid," the curator said as we ambled aisle after aisle. "She looked for it when she was here once. Keep an eye out." I had read Pam's book *Esperanza Rising* during my teaching career.

Did Marguerite inspire Pam to be a writer too?

I later emailed Pam to ask. I didn't get to write Marguerite, but because of Marguerite, I had the courage to write another beloved children's author. Pam replied that her horse books *Paint the Wind* and *Riding Freedom* were a nod to *King of the Wind*.

That afternoon in the reading room of the Elmer L. Andersen Library it hit me: it didn't matter that I had never sent a letter to Marguerite Henry despite her address being tucked away in my desk drawer for years. I had not lost an opportunity to get to know my favorite author. In fact, I had gotten to know her on an even deeper level than I probably ever would have in receiving a single letter from her. I thought about Margo and her personal mission to deliver a birthday card to Penny Chenery, and realized I'm not alone in wanting to reach out to know and be known by a heroine. I had been on a personal mission to find Marguerite, not just for myself, but for myriad folks, young and old alike, who still love her. She brought sweet, uplifting stories into the world, and I believe with all my heart the world still needs sweet, uplifting stories. Perhaps even more so than in Marguerite's heyday.

I came across a letter in the archive that wonderfully expresses these feelings I had but were so swirled, I could not articulate them clearly. The letter penned to an eighty-three-year-old Marguerite read, "I was one of those children you wrote for in the past. I think that loving and caring for animals develops traits in a child's character of kindness and understanding for all life on this Earth. For me, as I am sure it is with many others, your stories live past a fleeting fascination of youth and become an integral part of one's being."

Marguerite's stories had become a part of my being!

I will never possess Marguerite's prodigious talent, but by knowing who she was and what she was like, perhaps I can emulate her to some small degree. Midway through writing this book I started keeping a file folder system like she did. Instead of labeling each file with black crayon, I used a Sharpie. Had I employed her research techniques to my process earlier, perhaps this book would have been completed like hers, in the time it takes a mare to carry and bring a foal into the world. Regardless, just as a mare carrying a foal gives hope to the horse people who love her and have big dreams for the offspring on four hooves, getting to know Marguerite, hunting down sources for facts, corralling details about her, and choreographing words on a page gave me hope and a purpose.

I got to know Marguerite by reading her letters to legions of fans. Along the way, I made incredible acquaintances and met her in-real-life friends. I met Ed Richardson, the man who, as a little boy, rode Misty after school in the 1950s. I spoke with Matt, the man behind MistysHeaven.com who wants to have an online space for Misty fans to see pictures of Misty's family that makes them happy. I met Kendy, the retired librarian committed to preserving the Misty line of Chincoteague Ponies. I befriended Amanda and Rebekah of the International Chincoteague Pony Registry and Association, who are trying to keep lineage records while promoting the breed. Rebekah introduced me to her palomino pinto Chincoteague Pony named Pixie who carried me around during a dreamlike ride.

Also, during my research and writing, I met someone who I believe is my Sidney. He traveled with me to the lakeside destination where one hundred years ago Marguerite met and fell in love with the kind man from Wisconsin she shared a life with for sixty-four years. This man, also kind and from Wisconsin, drove me to the sites in Milwaukee where Marguerite grew up and attended school. He has offered unwavering support for my curiosity, research, travels, and writing. And unlike my ex-husband, who never got around to reading my blog posts, articles, and books, this man listened as I read chapters aloud and even asked me if he could read this manuscript.

While searching for Marguerite's backstory, I encountered her word play, penciled cursive notes strewn on narrow strands of paper, backs of envelopes, and yellowed typing paper. I studied both her research and writing techniques and can now try to mirror her ways. I feel like the fan who wrote to her on October 20, 1993: "I am a writer too and have so much to learn from craftsmen like you. Maybe by the time I'm ninety I'll have a portion of your skill!"

I am still learning from her practices.

I uncovered behind-the-scenes stories about Marguerite and Misty that never made it into any of her books from *Auno and Tauno* to *Brown Sunshine*. There were so many back stories they won't all even fit into one book. (Many more of them you can find on my blog Saddle Seeks Horse.)

Although I never dropped a letter addressed to Marguerite in a mailbox, I "met" Marguerite again and again while writing this book. Instead of dwelling on my lost opportunity, I realized I need to celebrate what I gained through Marguerite, my muse. Through this woman who loved children and horses, I found adventure, friendship, pony joy, and an island haven. Pony Penning is months away at the time of this writing, and its magnetism is wooing me back. I will return next time with a circle of Chincoteague Pony friends (and much stronger mosquito spray).

I met Marguerite on charming Chincoteague, a destination I had so long held in my imagination, and it exceeded my expectations through its warm locals, laughing birds, and shimmering waters. And, of course, the wild ponies.

This letter from a fan sent thirty years ago to a ninety-one-year-old girl who loved horses captured the spirit of everything that Marguerite Henry meant to me as a child and still means to me today. "Mrs. Henry, your name is synonymous with love, beauty, passion, integrity and courage. I am so grateful to God for your books; and to you for responding in the concreteness of the literature you have taken the time to write ... I have felt many, many things while reading your literature, but never sorry, bored or disappointed. Always I feel moved to do greater things in my life."

I never met her, nor sent her a letter, but I found Marguerite, my muse, and so much more.

As I've reflected on the pony swims to and from Chincoteague, the foal auction, the Monday morning beach walk, and all that I learned about Marguerite; I knew that if she were alive today I would handwrite on pretty horse stationery a letter of thanks and mail it. It would go like this:

Dear Marguerite,

I have been a fan of yours for as long as I can remember. Thank you for bringing so much joy into my life through the pages of Misty of Chincoteague, and really all of your books. I feel as though we are kindred spirits, as I love libraries too. In fact, I grew up reading and borrowing your horse books from the Gail Borden Public Library where you used to do research. Small world. Your books have inspired me to be a lifelong reader, and for that I am grateful.

Also, you and I have something in common: Wayne! I learned how to ride on a borrowed Quarter Horse named Jim Dandy, who was an old field hunter owned by my parents' friend Cindy who lived on Dunham Road. I'll never forget going for a swim with Jim, a bright chestnut, in the quarry not far from Mole Meadow. When I finally got the horse of my dreams when I was in my twenties, I showed him and won Reserve Champion at a hunter/jumper show held across the street from what was then called Dunham Woods, right down the street from your Mole Meadow home. I owned and loved DC for sixteen years until he died of colic. I was horseless for several years, and then I found my handsome Knight. Literally. My dark bay Thoroughbred's name is Tiz A Knight, sired by Tiznow, the only horse to have won the Breeders' Cup Classic twice.

Words can't describe how much I love Knight and what a true friend he has been to me in the eight years we've been together. I want to be a better horsewoman with each passing day, so that I always do right by Knight.

Although I'm an adult, I still want to grow up to be like you. I want your A++ creativity, your tireless work ethic and unwavering optimism. Thank you for welcoming us, your readers, into the world of horses, especially when we had no way to get to a barn to know and love them firsthand. You made sure all of your fans felt like Misty belonged to them, just as we belonged to her and to each other. Oh, how I wish your generous spirit was more mainstream in the horse world of today. I will ponder what I can do to be more like you and more like Cindy, extending horses to the next generation.

Because of you, Marguerite, I have befriended many fellow horse and pony lovers I would have never met were it not for the story of a pretty pinto who once roamed an island. Thank you, Marguerite. I'm so grateful for all you've taught me and for who you are.

Sincerely,

Your Number One Fans,

Susan & Knight

"Go on and dream your own wonderful sequels."

Marguerite Henry wrote these words on a scrap of paper.
It's in Folder 3 Box 27 in the Kerlan Collection
at the University of Minnesota.

Notes

(LA) American Library Association Archives, University of Illinois
(GRHC) Grand Rapids History Center, Grand Rapids, Michigan
(HFP) Harvey Family Papers, Newberry Library, Chicago, Illinois
(MCHS) Milwaukee County Historical Society, Milwaukee, Wisconsin
(MHC) Marguerite Henry Collection, Kerlan Collection, University of Minnesota
(MHP) Marguerite Henry Papers, DuPage County Historical Museum, Illinois
(RMC) Rand McNally Collection, Newberry Library, Chicago, Illinois
(SCPL) St. Charles Public Library, St. Charles, Illinois

CHAPTER 1: WRITING MARGUERITE
I remember it yesterday": Laura Murry Interview, June 14, 2021.
Cindy, a friend of my parents: Read the tribute to Cindy, the horsewoman who opened the world of horses to me in real life on my blog at https://saddleseekshorse.com/tribute-to-my-horse-riding-patron

CHAPTER 2: BREITHAUPT BEGINNINGS
***Story of a Book*:** The short 1980 educational film was distributed to schools so teachers could show students that even famous authors have to go through several drafts of their writing. In one fan letter Marguerite

wrote, "Think of it! Fifteen minutes of acting, but days, weeks and even months to film. And the days were not just 9 to 5, but 7 a.m. to 10 p.m. As a kid, I yearned to be an actress, but not anymore."

"Bonnie was also a bucker and bolter.": With the help of the Milwaukee County Historical Society, I tracked down several locations of liveries in the neighborhood where Marguerite grew up. During the early 1900s, cars and horses both provided transportation.

I weighed nothing at all: "Family Notes." MHC Box 22 Folder 8.

picked it up very gingerly: Rough Draft for *About the Author* MHC Box 2 Folder 11.

Editors could be wrong, but not Gertrude": Marguerite Henry, *Junior Book of Authors*. Edited by Stanley J. Kunitz and Howard Haycraft. 2nd ed. H. W. Wilson Company, 1951.

printer's ink got into my blood: *The Daily Journal*. "Her Love of Printed Word Is Shared with the Young," September 9, 1988.

small words in a small voice: Letter to Bay Shore Union Free School District. MHC September 1993. Box 8 Folder 15.

who could glide without wings: Marguerite Henry, *Junior Book of Authors*.

They were working too: Rough Draft for *Something About the Author* MHC Box 2 Folder 11.

***The Delineator* July and August 1914:** accessed from the University of Pennsylva's online archives https://onlinebooks.library.upenn.edu/webbin/serial?id=delineator.

encouraged her youngest to participate: Marguerite Henry, *Junior Book of Authors*.

"in a wilderness of trees": Rough Draft of *Something About the Author* MHC Box 2 Folder 11.

"My hobby is words": Ibid.
rheumatic fever from the ages 10-12: 1968 MH Interview on YouTube https://www.youtube.com/watch?v=gEJIb6JHpoE&t=189.
"wrassling wildcats with Dan'l Boone": Rough Draft of *Something About the Author* MHC Box 2 Folder 11.
"signs on the gates of heaven": Ibid.
"saving the human race": Ibid.
"frisk about everywhere in wild abandon": Ibid.
a public swimming pool: Bobby Tanzilo, "Urban Spelunking: Diving into the History of Milwaukee's Natatoria." *On Milwaukee.* January 16, 2018. https://onmilwaukee.com/articles/milwaukee-natatoriums.
never got published: Charles Hillinger, "Horse Lovers' 'Dear Abby'" *Los Angeles Times*, November 11, 1979.
***The Mercury* and *The Echo*:** MCHS. *The Mercury* 1917-1920 (high school) and *The Echo* 1921-1922 (college) yearbooks.

CHAPTER 3: LOVE IN A PINE FOREST
Charleston craze: "Music Played in the 1920s" https://www.thepeoplehistory.com/20smusic.html.
met Marguerite's parents: David R. Collins, *Write a Book for Me: The Story of Marguerite Henry* Morgan Reynolds Incorporated,1999.
fashionable flapper: *The Milwaukee Journal*, engagement notice April 29, 1923.
mother of the bride and groom wore black: "Brilliant Wedding of Sidney C. Henry and Miss Breithaupt," *The Sheboygan Press Telegram* (Sheboygan, WI), 9 May 1923, Wed, p. 6.
Hotel Astor in downtown Milwaukee: Bobby Tanzilo, "Urban Spelunking: The Astor Hotel." *On Milwaukee*, April 13, 2021,

https://onmilwaukee.com/articles/astor-on-the-lake.

Al Capone was onto it: John R. Schmidt "Uptown, Past and Present." WBEZ Chicago, 13 May 2013, https://www.wbez.org/stories/uptown-past-and-present/beda1254-563a-474a-b4eb-f4d9f778da8c.

CHAPTER 4: A JOURNALIST'S JOURNEY

"all I could do was write": Kathleen Burns, "Meet DuPage Author Marguerite Henry, and Her 'Misty.'" *The Chicago Tribune*, November 25, 1968.

at the time of construction: "American Furniture Mart." *Chicagology*, https://chicagology.com/skyscrapers/skyscrapers001/.

"I could take notes!": Marguerite Henry, "Adventures of a Ghost Writer." *Writer's Digest*, Oct. 1935.

Boiling things down ever since": Kathleen Burns, "Meet DuPage Author Marguerite Henry, and Her 'Misty.'" *The Chicago Tribune*, November 25, 1968.

are selected with careful taste": Marguerite Henry. "Ornamental Lamps, Well Placed Add Beauty and Restfulness." *Photoplay*, May 1925.

inspired by Hollywood sets: Marguerite Henry, "Use Picture Ideas to Beautify Your Own Home at Very Small Cost." *Photoplay*, April 1925.

Write she must!": Marguerite Henry, "Adventures of a Ghost Writer." *Writer's Digest*, Oct. 1935.

Can do naught but see her": Ibid.

I joined the swarm": Ibid.

article to a home and garden magazine: Ibid.

your verbs conveyed action": Ibid.

foaming stein of beer:" Ibid.

in that era would be about $250 today: Thanks, Carolyn, for calling

Eastman Kodak to uncover that fact.
she'd heard no's before: Marguerite Henry. *Something About the Author*. 1988. MHP.
Clarence Darrow: Ibid.
helped Sidney write sales bulletins: Melinda Miller. Rand McNally & Company Press Release. February 18, 1949. MHP.
acclaimed illustrator who lived nearby: Gertrude B. Jupp, "My Little Sister Marguerite Henry." *Horn Book Magazine*, January-February 1950.
young things, human or otherwise": Ibid.

CHAPTER 5: A BOOK, AN ARTIST AND A PONY
Lost dozens of their personal herd: "The True Tale of Misty, Stormy, and Maybe the Worst Nor'easter of Them All - Misty of Chincoteague." *Secrets of the Eastern Shore*, Feb 19, 2015.
reestablish the herds over on Assateague Island: *Letter to Doris Sutherland*. April 4, 1962. MHC Box 22.
paid for it or not": Marguerite Henry. *The Illustrated Marguerite Henry: With Wesley Dennis, Robert Lougheed, Lynd Ward, and Rich Rudish*. Rand McNally, 1980.
book publishing dream team: National Sporting Library Exhibit, *Storied Friends*. July 2022. Middleburg, Virginia
owned by collectors today: Abby Beall, "Wesley Dennis." *The Art of Wesley Dennis*, http://wesleydennis.com/.
silky as milkweed floss: Mary Daniels, "Misty, the Horse That Belongs to Every Child." *The Chicago Tribune*, October 9, 1977.
shipped the right foal: Marguerite Henry, *Corrected Typescript Research Notes*. MHC Box 2 Folder 1.

I loved Marguerite Henry!": Mary Jon "Jonnie" Edwards Interview August 13, 2021.

I'd be there for her": Marguerite Henry, *A Pictorial Life Story of Misty*. Rand McNally, 1976.

the rain stopped, and we slept": Ibid.

the state of Virginia: Corrected Typescript Research Notes. MHC Box 2 Folder 1.

attendees was 6.5 years old: *Misty Birthday Party Scrapbook*. July 1948. MHC Box 15.

the pony was too green: Interview, Mary Jon Quayle Edwards.

unusually nice human being: "Marguerite Henry Ad." *Chicago Daily Tribune*, November 11, 1951.

CHAPTER 6: MOLE MEADOW AND MARY ALICE

At once attractive and frightening": Mary Alice Jones letter to Bennet Harvey, September 15, 1944. HFP Box 8 Folder 104.

To suck in lungsful of air": Marguerite Henry, *Henry*. Rand McNally & Co., 1969.

Misty of Chincoteague was born:" Marguerite Henry speech. "*Who Carry Umbrellas*" American Library Association, 1961,

best-selling author, Marguerite Henry": Bennet Harvey, *Information Concerning the Death of Mary Alice Jones*. September 30, HFP Box 8 Folder 104.

share the richest nuggets of their past": Marguerite Henry, "Horse Sense is Stable Thinking," *The Wayne-DuPage Hunt: A Chronicle of Events 1928-1980. Edited by Robert L. Sirotek, The Wayne-DuPage Hunt, 1980*.

prepared a Viennese dinner: Ibid.

more fun than any Berlitzer": Ibid.
horses and hounds: Marguerite Henry Interview by Roy Porter of Rand McNally, July 1961.
fluttering frames open: 16mm Home Movie. MHC, Box 28 Folder 4.
into an antique shop: Pat Gerlach, "Antique Hunting in the Fox River Valley." *Daily Herald* (Arlington Heights, IL) September 27, 1986.

CHAPTER 7: FILE FOLDERS, PAPER SCRAPS AND WRITER'S CRAFT

I like animals": Marguerite Henry, *Dear Marguerite Henry*.
source of wonder and challenge": Brian Mooar, "Misty Author Marguerite Henry Dies at 95." *The Washington Post*, November 27, 1997.
a quick visual outline: Gertrude B. Jupp, "My Little Sister Marguerite Henry." *Horn Book Magazine*, January-February 1950.
animals in her books: *Untitled Research Notes for Justin Morgan*. MHC Box 19.
after Marguerite has described them": Wesley Dennis, *Tribute to Marguerite*. MHC Box 29 Folder 4.
the more you read, the better you write: Marguerite Henry, *Something About the Author*.
she simply tells what happened: Fanny Butcher, "Unknown." *The Chicago Tribune*, December 6, 1967. MHC.
the writer or his book: James Playsted Wood, "The Honest Audience." *The Horn Book Magazine*, October 1967. MHC.

CHAPTER 8: RESEARCH, LIBRARIES AND LIVING THE STORY

the perfect connotation: Alberita R. Semrad, "Marguerite Henry,

Newbery Medal Winner." *Publishers' Weekly*, March 26, 1949.

postcard of Independence Rock: Independence Rock Folder. MHC Box 20 Folder 1.

the actual writing: *Letter to Mary Alice Jones,* October 20, 1967. MHC Box 16 Folder 15.

you are transported into the past": *Marguerite Henry Newsletter No. 6.* Spring 1968. SCPL.

in those long ago diaries": Ibid.

around in the stacks for more": Marguerite Henry, *Album of Horses.* Rand McNally, 1951.

with encouragement and faith": *Untitled Document 3 Reasons Marguerite Loved Libraries.* MHC Box 13 Folder 11.

we have come to find ourselves": Ibid.

splendors of the ride": Marguerite Henry, *Something About the Author.* 1988. MHP.

know how it would taste": Marguerite Henry, *Dear Marguerite Henry.* Rand McNally & Co., 1969.

like a headless turtle": Ibid.

traveled to Italy three times": *Marguerite Henry Newsletter No. 5.* Leaf Raking Time 1967. SCPL

fitted neatly into place": Marguerite Henry, *Dear Marguerite Henry.* Rand McNally & Co., 1969

as though I had lived it myself": Marguerite Henry interviewed for Rand McNally by Roy Porter, July 1961.

CHAPTER 9 STORY FEEDBACK FROM THE SADDLE

picture a scene as if they were right there": *Letter to Mr. Merrit,* February 25, 1976. MHC Box 27 Folder 10.

like caressing the words": Marguerite Henry, *Dear Marguerite Henry*. Rand McNally & Co., 1969.

CHAPTER 10 THE STRUGGLE OF BRIDLING PEGASUS

you couldn't be happy doing anything else": *Marguerite Henry Newsletter No. 4*. April 1967. SCPL

wrote Marguerite back: 1961 speech to the American Library Association, *Who Carry Umbrellas*. MHC Box 22 Folder 11. This transcript of this speech was empowering to me as a writer, and I marveled at how smart it was to reach out to the very best in the field to learn their ways. How much dedication it took to locate the addresses of the writers and type (on a typewriter—and I read somewhere she was not an efficient typist) all the letters and mail them out and then wait for the replies. It must have been a gratifying mail day when she received each response.

machine gun of ideas": Marguerite Henry, "Adventures of a Ghost Writer." *Writer's Digest*, Oct. 1935.

not work in solitude": Marguerite Henry, *Dear Marguerite Henry*. Rand McNally & Co., 1969.

CHAPTER 11 THE PINNACLE OF SUCCESS

twenty-ninth published book: Margaret M. Clark, "Newbery and Caldecott Award Winners." *ALA Bulletin*, April 4, 1949.

encourage good writing in the field: Taylor Hartz, "100 Years of the Newbery Medal." *American Libraries*, June 2022.

as modest as Marguerite Henry!": Alberita R. Semrad, "Marguerite Henry, Newbery Medal Winner." *Publishers' Weekly*, March 26, 1949.

well enough to buy it": Melinda Miller. Rand McNally & Company Press Release. February 18, 1949. MHP.

I read in disbelief": Marguerite Henry, *A Pictorial Life Story of Misty*. Rand McNally, 1976.

department store Herpolsheimer's: "Librarians Plan Meet." *The Grand Rapids Press*, October 26, 1949.

make her feel at ease": Marguerite Henry, *A Pictorial Life Story of Misty*. Rand McNally, 1976.

a letterhead and a wish": Marguerite Henry, "Newbery Acceptance Paper." *The Horn Book Magazine*, January-February 1950.

I accept the Newbery Medal": Ibid.

taken by *The Grand Rapids Press*: Misty photo taken at the banquet hall, *The Grand Rapids Press*. GRHC.

even lifted a finger to get her there": Virginia Chase, *Letter to Helen Kinsey*. November 29, 1949. ALA.

Misty was a huge success": Helen Kinsey, *Letter to Virginia Chase*. December 1, 1949. ALA

children who crowded the store": Alberita R. Semrad, "Marguerite Henry, Newbery Medal Winner." *Publishers' Weekly*, March 26, 1949.

***The Little Fellow* has just gone into a Spanish edition":** Gertrude B. Jupp, "My Little Sister Marguerite Henry." *Horn Book Magazine*, January-February 1950.

boast to all the neighborhood about my little sister!": Ibid.

cleaning the stable and currying Misty": Ibid.

CHAPTER 12 FAN MAIL AND FRIENDSHIP

Gertrude would reply to fan mail on her behalf": *Gertrude Jupp Letter*. March 9, 1968. MHC. Box 23 Folder 13.

She was the real thing": Bonnie Shields, February 11, 2022.

CHAPTER 13 INFLUENCE BEFORE INFLUENCERS WERE A THING

grandsires and great grandsires": Marguerite Henry, *Letter to Mary Alice Jones*. October 20, 1967. MHC, Box 16 Folder 15.

created the Spanish Mustang Registry: *Wyoming Cowboy Hall of Fame*, https://www.wyomingcowboyhalloffame.org/robert-bob-brislawn.

we wrote out our checks": Marguerite Henry, *Letter to Sanford Cobb*. November 3, 1967. MHC Box 20.

all the children of the earth it is you": Marguerite Henry, *Letter to Bob Brislawn*. October 4, 1967. MHC Box 20 Folder 12.

public to get to know": MHC Box 20.

a buckskin she named Yellow Wings: Marguerite Henry, *Letter to Bob Brislawn*. April 1, 1968. MHC Box 20 Folder 13.

"destroy" was inserted in its place: Marguerite Henry, "Rewriting: I Do It My Way." *California English*, November-December 1982, MHC Box 10 Folder 13.

research on Clydesdales for *Album of Horses*: Marguerite Henry, *Andy Haxton Telephone Interview Transcript*. MHC Box 2 Folder 1.

I am planning to mention the places": Marguerite Henry, Letter to Roland Lindemann. 1960. MHC. Box 2.

New York Zoological Gardens: Marguerite Henry, *All About Horses*. Random House, 1962.

Eddie the Elegant Elephant: *Rand McNally Eddie the Elephant at Marshall Fields*. RMC Box 24 Folder 380.

she has to have a little handout of oats": "Album of Horses Interview." *Feature Foods Program*, Radio Broadcast, WLS, November 12, 1952. MHC Box 28 Folder 1.

enjoy looking them over": Marguerite Henry, *A Pictorial Life Story of Misty.* Rand McNally, 1976.
pony birthday party: *16mm Misty Birthday Party.* MHC Box 28 Folder 3.
brought down the house": Marguerite Henry, "Horse Sense is Stable Thinking," *The Wayne-DuPage Hunt: A Chronicle of Events 1928-1980.* Edited by Robert L. Sirotek, *The Wayne-DuPage Hunt, 1980.*
plight of the wild ones": Bob Brislawn, *Letter to Marguerite Henry.* March 8, 1968. MHC.
ask that the law enforcers uphold it": *Marguerite Henry Newsletter No. 4.* April 1967. SCPL
has brought a big victory": *Marguerite Henry Newsletter No. 7.* Autumn 1968. SCPL
wild horse so important to western history": Ibid.

CHAPTER 14 CHINCOTEAGUE PONY SUPERFANS

It all started with Marguerite": Allison Dotzel Interview, July 2, 2022.
map of the U.S. on her withers": *The Dynasty of Misty Note.* MHC Box 15 Folder 12.
Facebook page DSC Photography: Darcy Cole Interview, July 7, 2022.

CHAPTER 15 PONY PENNING PRELUDE

Misty of Chincoteague, **it's a dream of a story":** Cindy Faith led the Chincoteague Step Through Time Tours (I participated in two walking tours) during Pony Penning Week 2022. One tour was of the historic downtown, highlighting the unique past and culture of Chincoteague

Island, the other was held at the Beebe Ranch. At the time of this writing, the ranch was just purchased by the Museum of Chincoteague; the museum will keep the history of Misty alive. I did not get to do the Step Through Time pirate tour, but hope to in the future. Arrr!

CHAPTER 16 SWIMMING PONIES AND WINNING PONIES
Kendy had read all the Marguerite Henry books: Kendy Allen Interview, September 13, 2022. In the early 2000s, Kendy wrote books about Misty Family Ponies and Swim Veteran Ponies: *Misty's Black Mist and the Christmas Parade, Misty's Heart of the Storm,* and *Ember's Story: the Misty Miracle Pony.*

I determined to meet the author in person": Charles Hillinger. "Introduction," *The Illustrated Marguerite Henry.*

CHAPTER 17 THE MISTY MYSTIQUE
Misty's a pivotal part of my life": Matt DesJardins Interview, August 12, 2022. If you haven't visited MistysHeaven.com, the website Matt started to provide information about Misty and her descendants, take a gander. There are loads of photos, articles and family trees. And the site is continually updated. For example, in late May of 2023, a woman connected with Misty's Heaven and provided photos and background information about Wings, the pony who sired all three of Misty's foals.

CHAPTER 18 A TRIUMPHANT LIFE
expanded our hearts to fill both": Marguerite Henry, *A Pictorial Life Story of Misty*

a tiny light in the surrounding gloom": Fred Rasmussen, "'Misty of Chincoteague' Tale Gallops on Horse: Marguerite Henry, Who Died

Recently, Wrote 59 Books, but Her Tale of Two Orphans and a Horse Remains a Breed Apart." *The Baltimore Sun*, December 27, 1997.

hardest thing I have ever done": Ibid.

submitting to smothering hugs": Marguerite Henry, Letter to Sandy Price, August 18, 1986. MHC Box 16 Folder 1.

never, never write at all": Marguerite Henry. "Misty Revisited." *Just About Horses*, Winter 1977.

scientists call it spontaneous combustion": *Marguerite Henry Newsletter No. 4*. April 1967. SCPL

totally devoured that book: Georgia Glynn, *Letter to Marguerite Henry*. March 29, 970. MHC Box 23 Folder 12.

a book for another publisher": Bennet Harvey, *Letter to Director of Colonial Williamsburg*. 1962. MHC Box 23.

I. . . keep thinking of him": Marguerite Henry, *Snowman Notes*. MHC Box 4 Folder 9.

get a hold on your heart strings": Mary Alice Jones, *Letter to Marguerite Henry*. September 15, 1957. MHC Box 16 Folder 15.

revealed the complicated answer: *Letters between Susan Knopf and Marguerite Henry*, 1987. Box 15 Folder 5.

here's looking at you kid": Tom Nebbia, *Letter to Marguerite Henry*. April 25, 1989. MHC Box 15 Folder 5.

His ashes were scattered at sea: Dale Leatherman, "Marguerite Henry: Forever Young." *Equus Magazine*, https://equusmagazine.com/horse-world/young021603/.

'But Sid, we are home'": Marguerite Henry, *Letter to Bennet and Dorothy Harvey*. Undated. HFP.

working on *Brown Sunshine*—and she was HAPPY!": Bonnie Shields Email. January 20, 2023.

memory to enfold it and a heart to love it'": Marguerite Henry, *Something About the Author*. 1988. MHP.
Relating to a horse makes us better people": Marek Oziewicz Interview. September 28, 2022.
"This note washes away all the work": Dina Stallings, *Letter to Marguerite Henry*. November 11, 1980. MHC Box 5.

CHAPTER 19 MARGUERITE MY MUSE
decorated with a sketch of a seahorse." Marguerite Henry, *Letter to Mr. and Mrs. Starn*. July 24, 1983. Miss Molly's Inn, Chincoteague Island, Virginia gave me a copy of the letter which they have on hand for guests.
It was too generous of praise": Marguerite Henry, Post-It Note on unpublished *Mini Horses*. 1987. Box MHC Box 15.
I like to be thought of in that way": "Album of Horses Interview." *Feature Foods Program*, Radio Broadcast, WLS, November 12, 1952. MHC Box 28 Folder 1.
popularity is not diminished since your heyday": Nancy Stenard, *Letter to Marguerite Henry*. January 22, 1995. MHC Box 25 Folder 5.
one of the hardest things she has ever had to do: Lee Galda Interview August 11, 2022.
Braille books: Norah Smaridge. *Famous Modern Storytellers for Young People*. Dodd, Mead & Company, 1969.
I feel moved to do greater things in my life": Lizabeth Hizey, *Letter to Marguerite Henry*. February 4, 1993. MHC Box 8 Folder 15.

Acknowledgements

I am grateful to the passionate pony people who shared their insights with me. Thank yous and sugar cubes to Tara Tibbets and Gene, Allison Dotzel and Finn, Darcy Cole and her camera, and Gina Aguilera of the Pony Names app. Thank you to my new friends and adventure lovers I met on Chincoteague: Margo, Jing, Lizzie and Bailee.

Author Carly Kade supported this dream from the start, and her enthusiasm buoyed me through early challenges. #authorsunite. Emily Esterson was the best book coach, developmental editor and encourager as I muddled through the middle. Hunt caps off to Holly Caccamise for spotting missing commas and rogue ellipses.

A Shire-sized thank you to Rebekah Hart from the International Chincoteague Pony Association and Registry for answering my breed questions, letting me ride Pixie and designing the charming Misty graphic at the end of this section. I frequently relied on the Misty's Heaven website created with love by Matt DesJardins and overseen in meticulous detail by Amanda Geci, also of the International Chincoteague Pony Association and Registry.

Thanks to Amanda, I met Kendy Allen and her daughter Kerra Johnson, who was the little girl who got to talk to Marguerite on the phone. Kendy's story and commitment to children and ponies is very Marguerite-esque.

I appreciate the Chincoteague Pony gotcha stories of Sydney Rivera, the girl who left California; Katrina Balding-Bills for letting me "interview" Cricket (and Sarah Hickner for making the introduction); Margo Gulbranson for sharing a meal and her incredible tale of meeting Penny Chenery; and Lauren Hoeffer for letting me quote her letter from Marguerite.

Two strong artistic women have played a huge role in this book: Bonnie Shields and Amy Ellison. Bonnie has built a decades-long, successful career based on the art of the mule. I can see why Marguerite chose her to illustrate *Brown Sunshine*. For as talented as Bonnie is with a pencil (or whatever medium she chooses), she is equally fun, funny and a great storyteller. I can't thank her enough. I was over the moon when Bonnie agreed to create original art for this book. My other artist friend who dreamed up this beautiful book cover and acted as a motivating life coach is my gal pal Amy Summer Ellison.

Speaking of artists—like Marguerite, my photographer Carolyn Rikje is a mighty fine Midwesterner. The photos of Knight and me were easier envisioned than done. Another Midwesterner, Abby Beall, shared fascinating content about her favorite artist: Wesley Dennis. Thank you both.

A castle-sized thank you goes out to Karen Armbrust of the Wayne Historical Preservation Society. Karen's encouragement and enthusiasm for this project and the ideas and resources she shared all along the way were brilliant. I'm grateful to Richard Beltz for reading my letter and sharing his Mole Meadow memories. And I am still humbled by the generosity of Ed "Eddie" Richardson, the Misty rider, who shared beautiful Marguerite stories, along with his homegrown tomatoes. Jackie Knoop is a star for helping me connect with the Wayne crowd. I'm grateful to

Betsy Bramsen, Jonnie Edwards, Sky Magary, Rob Reed, Barbara Lyon and Sydney Baldwin for their insights.

A heartfelt thank you to Misty of Chincoteague Foundation members Peter Stone, Alex Hubbs and John Giusti.

This book would not be here without the historians, librarians and archivists in many states who helped me unearth clues. I can see why Marguerite admired them so!

Thank you to Northern Illinois historian Sandra Machaj, who chauffeured my mom and me around McHenry and Lake Counties to show us Lake Pistakee. Thank you to Bonnie Margitan, Dan Scrobel and the Minocqua Museum in Wisconsin for piecing together evidence to find the spot where Marguerite and Sidney met. Archivist Steve Schaffer of the Milwaukee County Historical Society deserves accolades for helping me map out Marguerite's days as a girl, teen and college student in Milwaukee. I will never forget that giant Sanborn Map! Milwaukee writer and historian Bobby Tanzilo knew the whereabouts of the Baptist church where Marguerite and Sidney married. I referred to his "Urban Spelunking" features at On Milwaukee over and over.

A round of applause goes to Bing Crosby historian Amy Hartman, Cutter Clotfelter of the Rancho Santa Fe Historical Society, Liane Leist and Laura Murry. I also appreciate the help of Emily O'Brien of the DuPage County Historical Museum, Marge Edwards of the Dundee Historical Society, and Lulu Zilinskas of the National Cowboy and Western Heritage Museum.

I am grateful to K.T. Horning, formerly of the University of Wisconsin-Madison, for her 1949 Newbery Award information and leading me to Cara Setsu Bertram of the University of Illinois, who provided primary source documents from Marguerite's Newbery win.

Marguerite referred to librarians as "friendly teachers" and it's true. Many thanks go to Karen Wickman of the Naperville Public Library, Jennifer Bueche of the Gail Borden Library, and Jordan Cloud of the Grand Rapids History Center. Jamie Poorman of the Marshall Public Library in Illinois is my Marguerite MVP: Jamie owns a Chincoteague Pony, is a Marguerite historian, genealogy researcher, and was a beta reader of this manuscript.

I'm grateful to Ramona, Gail, Amanda, Mattie and Celia for reading early versions of *Marguerite, Misty and Me*, and Laura Zecchin-Guse, who translated the title of the Italian newspaper article into English. Thank you to Brian, for kayaking with me in Minocqua and listening as I read aloud bumpy chapters, seeking feedback. Your support is as deep as Lake Michigan, and I look forward to more dancing and kayaking in our future.

This book would never have come to fruition without the help of various team members of the University of Minnesota. Lisa Von Drasek, Curator of the Children's Literature Research Collections/Kerlan Collection at the University of Minnesota Libraries; Caitlin Moreau, Assistant Curator; Karen Hoyle, former Curator of the Kerlan Collection; Marek Oziewicz, Ph.D., D.Litt., professor of Literacy Education, and the Sidney and Marguerite Henry Professor of Children's and Young Adult Literature; and Lee Galda, the former Sidney and Marguerite Henry Professor of Children's and Young Adult Literature, provided insight, documents, guidance, stories, and treasure chests—I mean archival boxes—that allowed me to meet Marguerite and share her story.

And I'm so grateful for Ann Keckonen, Sidney Henry's distant relative for guiding me in the early stages of trying to discover MH.

Thank you and bear hugs to Uncle Milton for getting me started out on Ancestry.com, and to my mom, who always wanted a horse, for helping me pursue my riding and writing passions. I love you both.

Book Club Questions

1. Which Marguerite Henry books have you read? Which one is your favorite, and for what reason? If you have not read any of her books, what stories from your childhood captivated you?

2. Do you think *Misty of Chincoteague* would have become such a classic if Marguerite had partnered with an illustrator other than Wesley Dennis?

3. What facts or anecdotes about Marguerite's personal life or writing journey surprised you?

4. In the opening chapter, Susan shares how Cindy gave her an entry point into the world of horses with the opportunity to ride Jim Dandy. Who was your horse-world-entry point person? Have you been that person for someone else?

5. Marek Oziewicz, the Sidney and Marguerite Henry Professor of Children's and Young Adult Literature at the University of Minnesota, observed that relating to a horse makes us better people. In what way or ways have you found this to be true?

6. Susan closes *Marguerite, Misty and Me* with a letter to Marguerite. Have you ever written a fan letter? To whom, and did

the person reply to you? If you haven't but decided to, who would be the recipient and why?

7. What unwritten Marguerite Henry book sequel would you like to read? Would you ever consider writing it yourself as Marguerite encouraged readers to do?

A Note From Me to You

Do you have a Marguerite memory or a Misty moment to share? A pony or horse that's captured your heart? I'd love to hear your story—and see your photos! Post on Facebook or Instagram use #mistyandme and tag me @saddleseekshorse. Not into social media? Email me at: susan@saddleseekshorse.com

WANT MORE MARGUERITE?
For bonus stories, visit SaddleSeeksHorse.com. I'm also available to speak at schools, libraries, book clubs, or riding groups—either in person or via Zoom. Drop me a line and let's make it happen.

FREE GIFT FOR YOU
Are you a horse book lover too? I'd love to send you my list of 10 must-read titles—head to saddleseekshorse.com/books.
Tally ho and happy reading!
– Susan

P.S. Would you leave a review on Goodreads or Amazon? Reviews help more readers discover my book. And please tell a friend! Word-of-mouth is one of the best ways great stories get shared. Thanks!

About the Author

Susan, a former English and history teacher, shares her equestrian passion on her blog SaddleSeeksHorse.com. She also co-hosts the Barn Banter by Horse Illustrated podcast and writes for horse magazines. When Susan's not writing or speaking about Marguerite and Misty, she's trotting around on her horse Knight in Bull Valley, Illinois. Susan would love to do an author talk at your library, school or club. Send her an email at susan@saddleseekshorse.com or reach out via Instagram or Facebook at @saddleseekshorse.

10 *Must-Read* HORSE BOOKS
FOR HORSE LOVERS

Looking for your next favorite horse book?

Grab your FREE guide to some of my top picks!

Visit saddleseekshorse.com/books.

Enjoyed meeting Misty & Marguerite?

Share with a young reader today!

AVAILABLE NOW @ saddleseekshorse.shop

101 Writing Exercises for the Horse Lover

Unbridled Creativity is a writing and journaling activity book for all horse-loving ages.

AVAILABLE NOW @ saddleseekshorse.shop

LOVING HORSES CAME EASY.
DATING AND FINDING SOMEONE TO LOVE WAS HARD.

Trot along with Susan in her horse lover's dating memoir and you might fall for someone tall, dark and handsome — and 16.3 hands!

Horses Adored and Men Endured is a charming collection of dating fiascos and horsey tales.

AVAILABLE NOW ● saddleseekshorse.shop

Strands of Hope
How to grieve the loss of a horse

Through personal stories, interviews and practical tips, find strands of hope for the bereaved equestrian.

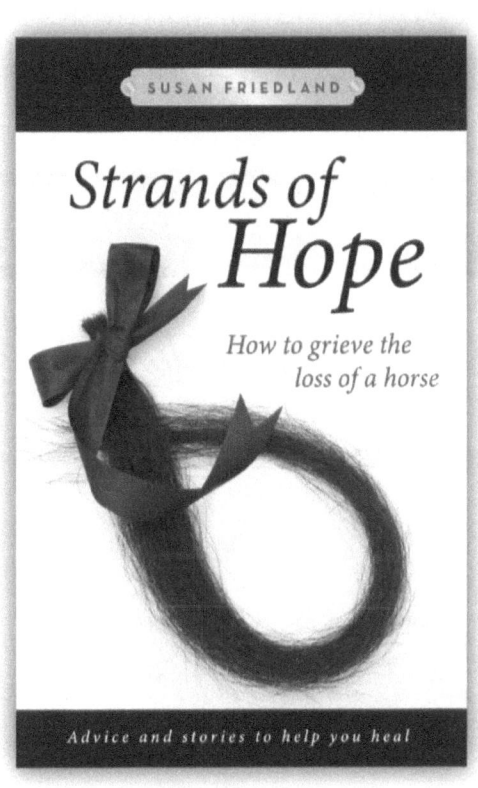

AVAILABLE NOW @ saddleseekshorse.shop

Let's Stay Connected!

You're invited to stay in the horsey loop with me.

Trot along on the blog where I share equestrian information and inspiration for horse lovers like us.

saddleseekshorse.com

Tally ho - Susan

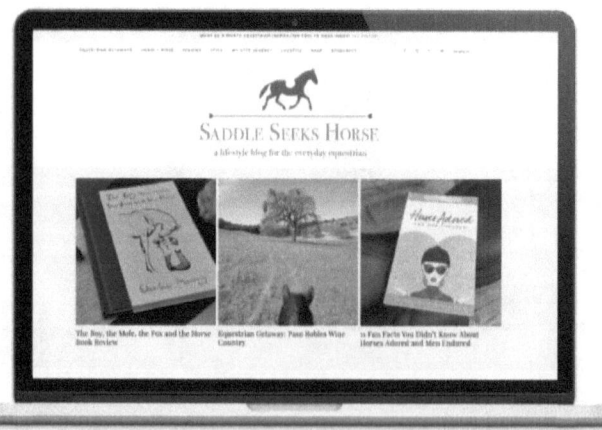

www.ingramcontent.com/pod-product-compliance
Lightning Source LLC
Chambersburg PA
CBHW030230100526
44583CB00013BA/683